Halls of Zion

Chapels and Meeting-Houses in Norfolk

by

Janet Ede, Norma Virgoe and Tom Williamson

'They stand, those halls of Zion,
All jubilant with song . . .'
(St Bernard, trans. J.M. Neale).

Centre of East Anglian Studies 1994

Acknowledgements

The Norfolk Nonconformist Chapels survey, and the publication of its results in the form of this book, would have been impossible without the help of a great many people. We would like to thank:

all those who so generously gave up their time to show us their chapels, houses or premises, and who provided us with invaluable information on the history of these buildings.

The volunteer recorders, whose names appear below, without whose help the survey would not have been possible.

Gillian Beckett	Valerie Belton
Richard Gordon Berry	John Bracey
Margery Catton	Julie Champeney
George Fenner	Jill Fletcher
Sophia Hankinson	Judy Hawkins
Trevor Heaton	Ted Hicks
J.Hodds	Peter Holman
Lesley Johnson	Ann Knight
John Knight	Diana Langran
Janet Lister	Karen Mackie
Wendy McGregor	John A.Mobbs
Tom Mollard	Sheila Mollard
Ivan Morris	Mary Muir
Jane Nolan	P.E.Page
Eustace Partridge	Brian Rumsey
D.M.Seaton	Brenda Stibbons
R.Southgate	Colin Tooke
M.E.Walker	Frances Warns
John Wright	

We would also like to thank the members of the Centre of East Anglian Studies at the University of East Anglia, especially the present Director Richard Wilson, his predecessor A. Hassell Smith, and Mavis Wesley.

Many of the photographs were provided by the members of the survey team, but additional ones were supplied by Eric Crane and Peter Raiswell, to whom special thanks are due. Thanks also to Phillip Judge for the maps and plans; to Frances Warns and Mary and Ian Muir for illustrations; and to Steven Hickling and Joyce Gurney Read for help with typing the results of the survey into the computer database. John Bracey supplied important information about the 'tin tabernacles'.

Staff at the Norfolk Record Office and Local Studies Library have given much help with documentary research.

The Norfolk Archaeological and Historical Research Group (previously Norfolk Archaeological Rescue Group) kindly provided the funds necessary for carrying out the Survey; Norfolk Museums' Service generously provided a grant towards the illustrations for this book; and the Centre of East Anglian Studies has borne the cost of its publication.

Finally, we would like to offer special thanks to George Fenner who did so much to organise and encourage the project.

The authors gratefully acknowledge the assistance of all these individuals and groups, and everyone else who contributed to the survey and to this book.

Census of Great Britain, 1851.

(13 and 14 Victoriæ, cap. 53).

A RETURN

OF THE SEVERAL PARTICULARS TO BE INQUIRED INTO RESPECTING THE UNDERMENTIONED

PLACE OF PUBLIC RELIGIOUS WORSHIP.

[N.B.—A similar Return will be obtained from the Clergy of the Church of England, and also from the Ministers of every other Religious Denomination throughout Great Britain.]

I.	II.			III.	IV.	V.	VI.	VII.			VIII.			IX.
Name or Title of Place of Worship	Where Situate; specifying the			Religious Denomination	When Erected	Whether a Separate and Entire Building	Whether used exclusively as a Place of Worship (Except for a Sunday School)	Space available for Public Worship			Estimated Number of Persons attending Divine Service on Sunday, March 30, 1851			REMARKS
	Parish or Place	District	County					Number of Sittings already Provided						
								Free Sittings	Other Sittings		Morning	Afternoon	Evening	
	(1)	(2)	(3)					(4)	(5)					
Independent Chapel	Fakenham	Heytor	Independent or Congregational Dissenters	1819	Yes	Yes	100	200	General Congregation	99	45	132	Morning service is usually attended by many persons from villages 12 to 5 miles distant; do cannot conveniently attend the other services	
										Sunday Scholars	28	32		
										Total..	127	77	132	
								Free Space or Standing Room for	Average Number of Attendants during months (See Instruction VIII.)					Afternoon chiefly domestic servants and agricultural labourers. Evening about half the congregation consisting of those not present at the preceding services.
									General Congregation				
									Sunday Scholars				
									Total ..				

I certify the foregoing to be a true and correct Return to the best of my belief. Witness my hand this __3rd__ day of __March__ 1851.

X. (Signature) ...... _William Legge_

(Official Character) _Minister_ of the above-named Place of Worship.

(Address by Post) _Fakenham_

One of the return forms from the Religious Census of 1851, relating to Fakenham Independent chapel. This is an example of the standard form for nonconformist places of worship. Note the remarks concerning the distances travelled by the congregation.

Introduction

In 1988 members of the Norfolk Archaeological Rescue Group (now the Norfolk Archaeological and Historical Research Group) became concerned that the county's rich heritage of nonconformist chapels and meeting-houses was under threat. Many were being demolished altogether, others drastically converted to new uses. Much antiquarian attention had, traditionally, been focused on Norfolk's Anglican churches, but a high proportion of the county's chapels and meeting-houses remained completely unrecorded. The group therefore decided to undertake a comprehensive survey of as many of the survivors as could be identified, whether these were still in use as places of worship, had been converted to new uses, or were unused and derelict. This book summarises the preliminary results of this programme of research.

As the survey progressed the magnitude of the task we had set ourselves became ever more apparent, with surveyors often finding two chapels, and sometimes even three or more, in a village. Thanks to the dedication and enthusiasm of the recorders over six hundred buildings were visited and their principal details are summarised in the gazetteer at the end of this volume. These buildings do not tell the whole story of non conformity in the county. Documentary sources, including the Licences for Places of Worship, the 1851 Census of Religious Worship and nineteenth-century directories, show that other chapels and meeting-houses once existed which have now entirely disappeared. Moreover, many of the buildings which we see in the landscape today, although perhaps very old, are themselves often replacements of yet earlier meeting places. Inevitably some chapels and meeting-houses will have been missed by the survey and the authors would be grateful for any information regarding unrecorded buildings.

Warham, Primitive Methodist. Overgrown and neglected: this is the fate of so many of the county's chapels. Yet at its inauguration in 1872, the Norfolk News reported that over two hundred people 'sat down to an admirable repast' at the public tea.

Dissent in Norfolk

Popular tradition claims that nonconformity has always been especially strong in East Anglia. Lollardy had some impact in the region in the late Middle Ages and Dissent – protest against the beliefs and practices of the Established Church – burgeoned here in the decades after the Elizabethan religious settlement. The compromise state church which Elizabeth and her advisers set up was considered unsatisfactory by those who demanded a more thorough-going Reformation on Continental lines. Most stayed within the Church of England and attempted to bring about change from within. Others, however, often with more fundamental objections, were driven out and set up separatist congregations.

The proximity of the Low Countries was a vital factor in stimulating early Dissent in Norfolk, for Holland acted as a refuge for believers in danger of persecution here. Moreover, the model of the Dutch Reformed church provided a stimulus to radical religious beliefs and encouraged the sturdy independence of individuals and congregations. Movement between East Anglia and the Low Countries became commonplace for those seeking freedom of belief. As early as 1581 Robert Browne set up a 'gathered church' in Norwich which was almost immediately forced to emigrate to Middelburg. Later, in the early seventeenth century, over fifty clergymen in the Diocese of Norwich were suspended by the zealous Bishop Wren. Their principal offence was that they had ignored Archbishop Laud's directions concerning the taking of communion and had refused to read from the pulpit King James' *Book of Sports*, reissued in 1633, which was intended to encourage athletic games and dances after Sunday worship and thus to counteract too strict an observance of the Sabbath. Some of these clergymen may simply have been Puritans pushed outwards from the mainstream of the Laudian religious order, but others may have entertained more radical beliefs. A number of these ministers fled to Holland and founded their own church there.

The upheavals of the Civil War and the Interregnum gave some religious exiles the opportunity to return home. William Bridge, who had become pastor of the Rotterdam church in 1638, returned in 1640 and founded a church at Yarmouth. Two years later members of this congregation, who had formerly travelled all the way from Norwich to attend meetings there, set up their own church at St George's, Tombland. Similar congregations were soon established elsewhere in the county.

The Interregnum was a time of considerable religious dispute. One party, the Presbyterians, wanted to maintain the discipline of a state church but purged of what they considered the remaining trappings of Popery. Others, however, believed in the creation of voluntary or 'gathered' churches and advocated a measure of toleration for different religious views. These 'Independents' were, however, themselves riven by internal disputes especially over the question of infant baptism. This issue led to the separation of the Baptist from the Independent churches. The Pulham congregation was perhaps the first group in Norfolk to insist on the baptism of adult believers only, a decision taken as early as 1646. In the same year the Wymondham congregation was split over this issue. The congregation at Ingham was also Baptist in outlook by the late 1640s, according to chapel tradition.

In the fervent atmosphere of the Interregnum other religious groups arose, most notably the Society of Friends, founded by George Fox. The 'Quakers', as they soon became known, first appeared in Norfolk in 1654. Thomas Symonds visited Cambridge gaol to mock a group of imprisoned Friends, but was convinced by their views and returned, transformed, to Norwich. Soon afterwards he was joined by other Quakers who settled in the city and formed a meeting at his house. Immediately persecution and imprison ment began, with fines harshly imposed upon their property and goods: even under the generally tolerant rule of Cromwell there was widespread hostility towards this group.

With the Restoration of the monarchy in 1660 and the triumph of the Church of England, all Dissenting groups were forced into hiding and suffered persecution. At Ingham the congregation is said to have met in a cottage around a table laid for a meal. The minister, disguised as a drover, would preach to the assembly from a shed adjoining the house and opening into it by means of a cupboard door, whilst watchers guarded the road outside.

It was not until the 1672 Declaration of Indulgence that worship by Dissenters was officially tolerated, although even then only on condition that their premises were licensed. Many of these licenses survive and can be used to provide some indication of the geographical distribution of Dissenting congregations in the county. They show that they were to be found at this time in Norwich, King's Lynn and Yarmouth; in a broad scatter in the north-east of the county; and as a smaller cluster in the Waveney valley in the south, an extension of a similar concentration of meetings over the county boundary in north Suffolk. This pattern was, to a large extent, the consequence of social factors. Both the north-east of the county and the south were areas in which there were few large estates or powerful landowners. The members of the minor gentry and the moderately well-off freehold farmers who characterised these areas were powerfully

The Old Meeting, Colegate, Norwich. The most sophisticated seventeenth-century meeting-house in Norfolk. Erected in 1693 by a wealthy urban Independent congregation, the building – with a facade ornamented with rows of pilasters surmounted with elaborate Corinthian capitals – is a proud statement of new-found toleration (Photo RCHME Crown Copyright).

attracted by the independence of mind of Old Dissent. In the north-east, Lessingham, Trunch, Bradfield, Northrepps, Tunstead and Lammas with Little Hautbois all had their Dissenting congregations: that which met in the kitchen of Irmingland Hall had, no doubt, once been supported by the owner, Lieutenant-General Fleetwood, son-in-law of Oliver Cromwell.

These groups did not meet in purpose-built chapels, but in cottages and private houses, in sheds and workplaces, in barns and stables and at Wymondham in 'the open yard of John Lawrence, gentleman'. They often changed their meeting places with some frequency: thus the Independent congregation in Norwich, ejected from St George's, Tombland at the Restoration, met in various private houses, a brewhouse, and then in the Blackfriars' Hall. With the passing of the Act of Toleration in 1689, however, purpose-built chapels began to appear, many in the principal towns and in the City of Norwich, others in more remote locations. The Norwich Independent

Denton Congregational chapel was built in 1821 on the site of an earlier building. It has the square plan, double entrance doors and plain elevation typical of early chapels: but the two porches with their elegant pillars bring a touch of sophistication to this remote building.

Morley High Oak Primitive Methodist chapel in Wicklewood was originally built as a house, and then became a public house, before being converted to a chapel.

congregation erected what is now known as the 'Old Meeting' in Colegate, a fine building which has remained largely unchanged since its construction in 1693. Guestwick Independent chapel still contains part of a 1690s building embedded within its present fabric. The Quakers, too, were building in this period, even before the passing of the Act. In 1670 they had bought land at the Guildencroft in Norwich for use as a burial ground; in 1679 they opened a meeting-house in Goat Lane; and in 1698 completed a second on the Guildencroft site. Another was built at Wymondham in 1687, to house a congregation which had formerly gathered in a ruined medieval chapel.

In the first half of the eighteenth century many Dissenting congregations declined or disappeared. There was a general cooling of the religious temperature. When the philosopher Montesquieu visited England in 1732 he observed that 'there is no such thing as religion in England. If one speaks of religion everyone begins to laugh'. The Presbyterians, in particular, dwindled in numbers and influence. Many joined the Unitarians, another group which had developed during the Interregnum. Unitarians rejected the doctrine of the Trinity and stressed the essential unity of God. Their insistence on an appeal to reason and personal conscience went hand in hand with a dedication to the cause of religious liberty. From the 1750s, however, a new vitality is apparent in English Dissent, and is manifested, for example, among the Independents by the writing and teaching of Philip Doddridge. In the south of Norfolk, new groups spread out from the old established centres, while a whole new cluster of congregations appeared in the centre-north of the county. By the time of the Religious Census of 1851, there were forty-nine Independent or – as they were now coming to be known – Congregational chapels in Norfolk. The Baptists, too, benefitted from this renewal: but the real growth in the late eighteenth and nineteenth centuries was in Methodism.

Left: Old Meeting, Norwich, Congregational. One of a rich collection of memorials in this city-centre chapel. Its classical design, marble pillars and urn are also to be found in Anglican churches of the early eighteenth century.

Right: Old Meeting, Norwich, Congregational. Expensive monuments are a public statement of the wealth and status of the family of the dead.

South Lopham Baptist chapel. Stylistically this would appear to be an eighteenth-century building, but so far no documentary evidence has been uncovered to confirm this.

In origin Methodism was an evangelical movement within the Established Church, but its leaders – the brothers John and Charles Wesley – were increasingly forced out by the indifference and hostility of the church hierarchy. A form of Methodism first appeared in the county with James Wheatley's arrival in Norwich in 1751. Wheatley had a chequered career. He began as one of Wesley's preachers but he was expelled from the movement, probably for selling quack medicines. He was later reinstated by a reluctant Wesley and came to Norwich where he attracted great crowds with his sermons preached in the Castle Ditches. Very soon a preaching-house, the Tabernacle, was set up on Timberhill. But violent anti-Methodist riots ensued which convulsed the city for some ten months: Wheatley was physically assaulted and the Tabernacle was torn down. With the re-establishment of public order, a new Tabernacle was built at St Martin's-at-Palace Plain, a huge building with an adjoining house for the minister, designed by the prestigious Norwich architect Thomas Ivory.

John and Charles Wesley first visited Norwich in 1754. Shortly afterwards, they rented a building known as the Foundry and established a Society which grew very quickly. Meanwhile, John Wesley was persuaded to take over the lease of the Tabernacle in 1759 following the public disgrace of Wheatley, who had been tried and convicted for immorality. Wesley was reluctant to accept responsibility for the congregation here, finding the members to be of 'unparalleled fickleness'. In 1763 he told the congregation

> *For many years I have had more trouble with this Society than with half the Societies in England put together.*

In fact, after only seven years he gave up the lease and the building was finally taken over by the Countess of Huntingdon and became part of her Connexion – a group of Calvinistic Methodists distinct from the followers of Wesley.

The Foundry congregation, however, continued to grow, and soon required larger and more permanent accommodation. A new chapel was built in Cherry Lane in 1769, with John Wesley contributing £270 to the construction costs. By the early years of the nineteenth century the congregation had become so large that a member described how 'every part of the chapel was crowded to excess and multitudes were obliged to go away for want of room'. In consequence, Calvert Street chapel was begun in 1809 and when the congregation still continued to grow, St Peter's Wesleyan chapel in Lady Lane was opened in 1824.

By this time other Methodist Societies had been established throughout the county by Wesley's itinerant preachers, although often in the face of bitter hostility and violence. Wesley himself travelled through Norfolk on numerous occasions and although he preached in many villages, he concentrated his efforts

North Lopham, Wesleyan Methodist. John Wesley preached under an ancient ash tree in North Lopham in 1758. The Society met subsequently in a kitchen and then in various barns. In 1810 the chapel was built and a day school was added in 1838.

Calvert Street Methodist Church, Norwich. This fine building, erected in 1810 to cater for the rapid expansion of the Methodist cause in the city, was demolished in 1966 to make way for the Magdalen Street flyover (Photo RCHME Crown Copyright).

principally on the main centres of population: Norwich, King's Lynn and Great Yarmouth. Following the pattern set by earlier Dissenting groups, the new Societies tended at first to meet in cottages, barns, workshops and industrial premises. Thus the kitchen at Grange Farm housed the first Methodist Society at North Lopham: a sailmaker's loft served the early congregation in King's Lynn: and a blacksmith's shop provided shelter for the first group of Methodists at Framingham Earl. In time, however, chapels were erected, although the limited funds available often meant that these were simply conversions of the original premises.

This pattern repeated itself when, following the death of John Wesley, successive groups broke away from the main body of Methodism, setting up their own congregations and rival structures of organisation. The group which eventually became known as the Primitive Methodists split from the parent body in 1809. The movement did not reach Norfolk until 1820, however, when the county was incorporated into the huge Nottingham Circuit, with missioners being sent to preach in King's Lynn. Not long after this they began to hold services on Mousehold Heath in Norwich: the natural auditorium they used for their camp meetings came to be known as 'The Ranters'

Hole'. A hayloft at St Augustine's was hired as their first chapel and this was soon followed by a host of other places of worship: Lakenham Old Chapel was built in 1823; Cowgate Chapel was converted from a brewery in 1840.

Primitive Methodist preachers were sent to Yarmouth in 1823 and they, too, rented a hayloft as their first meeting place. The congregations in and around the town were organised into a Circuit in 1825. Fakenham had also become a Circuit in 1823, King's Lynn in 1824 and by 1825 the Norwich Circuit had six ministers.

In 1826 a Yarmouth coal-heaver, Robert Key, experienced a dramatic conversion and soon afterwards began to work in central Norfolk as an itinerant preacher for the Primitive Methodists. At the outset he conducted services in cottages, but soon chapels were built for the growing congregations. Key later wrote of how he had established Societies at Reepham, Whitwell Street, Booton, Lenwade, Sparham, Hockering, North and East Tuddenham, Garveston, Bawdeswell, Shipdham, Saham Toney, Watton and Mattishall. The last he made the centre of the Circuit and from here the villages to the south were reached – Runhall, Barnham Broom, Whinburgh, Welbourne and Westfield. It is impossible to underestimate the importance of Primitive Methodism in the rural areas of Norfolk in the nineteenth century, especially as it became closely allied with the rising Trades Union movement among farm labourers. Indeed, union business was often conducted outside the chapel after the Sunday service. Nevertheless, the Primitives did not supplant the Wesleyans, who remained an important feature of Norfolk life.

Disagreements within the mainstream Wesleyan Methodist body resulted in a further bitter rift in 1849. The secessionists were known as Reformers, or in Norfolk (where they were particularly strong) as Wesleyan Branch. Sometimes entire congregations changed their allegiance, as at Calvert Street chapel in Norwich. In other instances, congregations split. The splinter group either met in temporary premises (at Lenwade they met at the King's Arms public house), eventually building a chapel of their own; or else the Reformers themselves were left in the old chapel, while the Wesleyan traditionalists moved away.

This, however, was the last major break in the movement. Thereafter the various branches of Methodism began to move towards each other again, beginning in 1857 with the formation of the United Methodist Free Church which embraced the Wesleyan Reformers and another breakaway group – the Wesleyan Reform Association. In 1932 almost all the Methodist groups were formally united. Mile Cross Methodist Church, Norwich, begun in 1933 and opened early in 1934, was widely seen as a tangible expression of this unity by the Norwich churches from the different traditions, each of which contributed money, manpower, expertise and support to its foundation.

Unlike Baptist and Congregational congregations which each supported its own minister and whose

In 1933 the architect Cecil Yelf designed Mile Cross Methodist church to serve the growing suburbs of north Norwich: a modern church incorporating fashionable art-deco details.

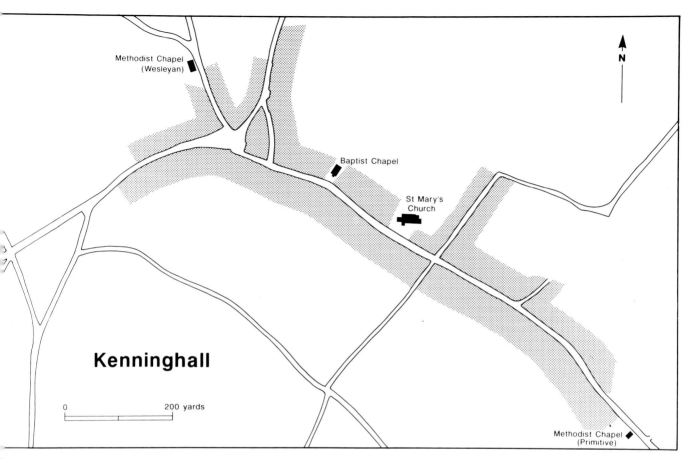

Methodist Chapel
(Wesleyan)

Baptist Chapel

St Mary's
Church

N

Kenninghall

0   200 yards

Methodist Chapel
(Primitive)

Kenninghall. The position of the Methodist chapels at the edges of the village beyond the immediate influence of the Established church is not unusual. Members of the congregation had to go out of the village – turn their backs upon it – to attend services. The array of chapels within a small settlement is a familiar feature in Norfolk.

minister and members travelled considerable distances or services, the circuit organisation of Methodism neant that only a few ministers were needed to cover a arge area, when ably supported by Local Preachers. Hence vast numbers of Methodist chapels were built, ach serving its own immediate locality yet all enjoying he benefits of links with a wider Connexion.

Methodism in all its forms was especially successful n Norfolk, far more so than the various older forms of Dissent. Indeed, apart from Lincolnshire, no other county in eastern England had such a proliferation of Methodist chapels. The various Methodist groupings peppered the county with their places of worship, many villages having two or even three. The tiny village of Sparham supported two Methodist chapels, whilst in 1851 Upwell parish contained three Wesleyan, four Primitive Methodist and three Wesleyan Reform chapels, as well as one for the Baptists.

The expansion of Methodism radically changed the map of nonconformity in Norfolk. But by the time the 1851 Religious Census was taken, other dramatic changes had occurred. Presbyterianism had now entirely died out after a series of doctrinal disputes, as a result of which most of its members had joined the Unitarians or the Independents. Quaker meetings remained at a low level, but all other branches of Old Dissent had multiplied in numbers, stimulated no doubt by the evangelical spirit of Methodism. In addition, new denominations had arisen. The Church of Latter Day Saints (the Mormons) reached its peak in 1851 with thirteen congregations, mainly in south-central Norfolk. Numbers declined dramatically after this, largely due to emigration of members to America, and it was not until the 1960s that they began to grow again.

In 1878 the Mission founded by William Booth became the Salvation Army and by the 1880s Salvationist groups were to be found in all the Norfolk market towns. There were also a few isolated congregations of Plymouth Brethren, mainly in north Norfolk.

Almost every parish in Norfolk had at least one nonconformist chapel by the close of the nineteenth century. The exceptions were almost invariably small or sparsely populated, like Bylaugh; immediately adjacent to towns well-endowed with chapels, like Hempton near Fakenham; or 'closed' parishes dominated by a single substantial landowner, like Sandringham.

Sheringham Salvation Army barracks, 1896.

The Location of Chapels

Many of the earliest chapels in the county are to be found in the principal towns and larger villages. Here they are usually set back from the street, half-hidden by other buildings, like Little Walsingham Methodist chapel (1793); or else, like Salhouse Baptist chapel (1802), tucked away and reached by alleys or lokes. Many others were built in remote locations away from the main centres of settlement, like the Baptist chapel in the small hamlet of Meeting Hill on the fringes of the parish of Worstead. Whilst such remote or secluded locations could not hide the building's existence from local hostility, a discreet rather than a blatant presence may have allowed a grudging toleration in the neighbourhood. Hostility there certainly was: as late as 1882 the struggling Methodist cause in Drayton complained of the 'bitter opposition' from the rest of the village.

Remote and secluded locations were not, however, always determined simply by a desire to keep a low profile. They might also result from the kinds of parcels of land which became available to congregations. Cheaper sites at the edge of the village, particularly the 'poor' end of the village, were more easily acquired as well as being more distant from the influence of parson and squire. Thus the Primitive Methodist chapel at North Elmham is surrounded by small cottages at the end of the village far from the church and the hall. It was cheapness, too, which explains the oddly-shaped sites often occupied by chapels. The triangular piece of land bought by the Wesleyan Methodists at Great Massingham resulted in an irregular, lozenge-shaped building; whilst at Lenwade a chapel was built with one corner cut diagonally in order not to impinge upon an adjacent public footpath.

Methodist Chapel, Little Walsingham, 1793. The earliest surviving Methodist chapel in Norfolk, hidden away down a loke behind the main building line. It is a striking structure nevertheless, with its round-arched windows, pedimented porch, and fine weather vane (Photo RCHME Crown Copyright).

Financing a New Chapel

There is little documentary evidence concerning the way in which the money to build the earliest chapels was raised, but it would seem that the same methods prevailed as were used in later years. The cost of building a new meeting place obviously depended upon its size, and by the nineteenth century a village chapel could cost anything from around £100 to well over £1000, a large town chapel several thousand pounds. Raising such sums required courage, resourcefulness and hard work, and chapel accounts and contemporary newspaper reports show that there were various ways in which building could be funded. Firstly there is some evidence that speculative builders put up chapels and offered them for rent. The Baptist chapel at Aylsham may have been built in this way in 1791, with the Baptists not actually buying it until some years later. Secondly, a congregation could be fortunate in having a benefactor willing to build the chapel at his own expense. At Thurne, for example, the Primitive Methodist chapel was built by a farmer, Mr H. Browne and in 1873

> being desirous that after his decease the Society should have a permanent place of worship he agreed to sell the chapel to the Connexion for £60, generously offering at the same time to give £30 if the other £30 could be raised by the congregation.

Thirdly, and most commonly, the congregation itself had to find the funds to buy the site and build the chapel. Trustees, legally responsible for all transactions, were appointed and fundraising begun. Bazaars, special sermons and tea meetings were organised and donations, including sums from other congregations in the area, were encouraged and sought. Frequently loans were taken out, but their repayment was painfully slow and debts often remained a source of worry for many years to come. In 1866 Diss Independent chapel celebrated clearing the debt which had been outstanding since 1835, while at Downham Market in 1866 the Wesleyans were again fundraising to make improvements to their chapel only two years after clearing the debt incurred in building it.

In 1908 the Primitive Methodists of Fakenham built a new chapel adjacent to the old building. Designed by A.F.Scott, it was built in memory of the Rev. H. Buckenham, born in Fakenham, who was the first Primitive Methodist missionary to Africa. Sixteen foundation stones record the names of donors.

It was advantageous to invite a high-ranking person to lay the foundation stone. At Langley the local squire, Sir Richard Proctor Beauchamp, officiated but in his speech he made it quite clear that though he had donated the site he was himself a staunch Anglican.

When building work started, the ceremony of laying the foundation stone provided another source of funds, since the person officiating was expected to place a donation on the stone. It was, therefore, helpful to invite a person of substance to perform this function. Names on the stones include MPs, JPs, local squires and prominent businessmen. As the century progressed the number of foundation stones tended to increase. The record must surely be held by the Primitive Methodist chapel at Lakesend in Upwell parish, built in 1914, which has no less than twenty-six foundation stones. It was also customary for villagers and Sunday school children to lay a brick, sometimes initialled, together with a suitable donation.

The Earliest Chapels

The earliest surviving chapels and meeting-houses in Norfolk – those dating from before 1750 – were mainly built for the Society of Friends (nine), with smaller numbers erected by the Independents (four) Baptists (two) and Presbyterians (two). They are mainly simple, rather 'vernacular' structures, rectangular in plan and with gabled and pantiled roofs. The majority have their doorways – usually two – set in one of the long sides; some have one or more internal galleries. Most of the surviving examples are built of brick, although the Presbyterian chapel at Hapton, erected in 1749, is timber-framed, and fragments of the original 1695 timber-framed building at Guestwick still survive, embedded in the nineteenth-century brick structure.

Lacking architectural pretensions, the overall style of most of these early buildings is close to that of contemporary farmhouses. Some, however, were more elaborate. To house bigger congregations, larger and squarer buildings were sometimes erected. Constructing a roof which could span such large voids

Hapton Presbyterian/ Unitarian chapel, built of timber and clay lump in 1749 (Drawing by M.Muir).

posed problems which in this period were usually solved by building double-gabled structures, with two parallel roofs side by side. The valley in between was supported by two massive internal pillars (sometimes jocularly referred to as 'Jachin and Boaz' after those in Solomon's temple). The Independent chapel constructed at Oulton in 1728 is a fine example of this kind of large imposing building, with its two doors, fine brick facade, and elaborate shaped gables. The most sophisticated meeting-house surviving from this period, however, is unquestionably the Old Meeting in Colegate, Norwich. The wealthy urban Independent congregation erected in 1693 a most accomplished building, its facade ornamented with rows of pilasters surmounted with carved Corinthian capitals, and with richly detailed canopies to the two doorways. No sign here of Puritan austerity. The building has not, however, survived entirely without alteration. Recent renovations have exposed evidence which suggests that the elegant sash windows may not be original, while the line of the roof was probably altered slightly during the eighteenth century.

Oulton Congregational chapel. Built in 1728, this is one of the earliest meeting-houses in Norfolk (Drawing by M. Muir).

The Interior of Oulton Congregational chapel before restoration.

18

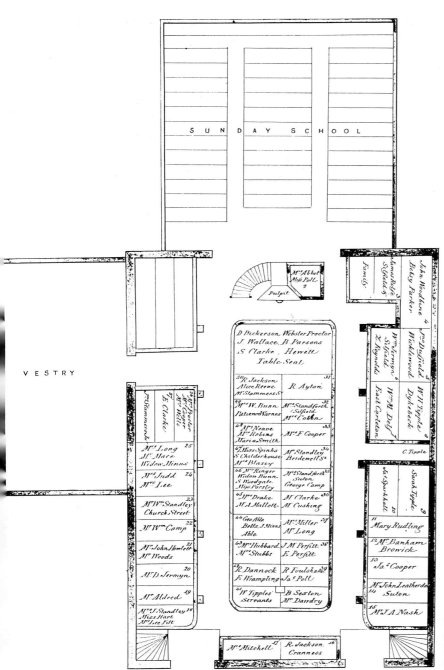

Wymondham Independent chapel. This plan of 1851 shows the arrangement of box pews before the building was extended and reseated in the 1870s.

Changing Styles, 1750 – 1820

The period after 1750 saw a substantial increase in the numbers of chapels being built and no fewer than fifty-four survive from the period up to 1820. The majority were associated with that new addition to the ranks of nonconformity, the Methodists. Their earliest surviving chapel, at Walsingham, was built in 1793; a further eighteen survive which were built in the decades up to 1820. The Baptists come a close second, with seventeen surviving structures from this period. Much smaller numbers were erected by the Friends (three). This is surely a reflection of the dwindling support for the movement at this time, something which also, in all probability, explains why so many of their earlier meeting-houses survive today, rather than having been demolished later in the century and replaced by more up-to-date buildings. The rest of our nonconformist heritage from this period is again made up of small numbers of chapels built by Presbyterians, Unitarians and Independents.

We do, however, need to be a little careful in assigning particular buildings to particular denominations since some are known to have passed from one denomination to another. This was possible because all denominations needed the same kind of building. Their main requirement was for a structure which allowed all those present to see and hear the preacher clearly. As a result, most meeting-houses had plans which were square or nearly so. But now, instead of spanning the roof with two parallel ridges, hipped roofs or more rarely pyramidal ones became normal

The Friends' meeting-house, North Walsham. A striking building of 1792. Inside the original seating still survives, little altered.

The Rev. John Alexander served first as Minister for the Countess of Huntingdon's Connexion at the Tabernacle in Bishopgate, Norwich. Following disputes there he moved to a small chapel nearby and finally in 1819 he founded the Congregational church at Princes Street and became its first Minister. It is not uncommon to find nonconformists moving from one denomination to another.

Smallburgh Baptist chapel. Supposedly built in the 1680s, the building has undergone many modifications at various times in the past: traces of some are visible in the brickwork of the facade shown here.

Most of the chapels built at this time also have galleries, which were either ranged along the side facing the pulpit (i.e. above the entrance doors, often with a vestibule beneath) or which ran around three sides of the building. These are supported on posts or pillars, sometimes with elaborate classical mouldings. The pulpit stands, or originally stood, in the centre of the opposing wall opposite the entrances, often raised high to command the galleries. These features are shared by the chapels used by almost all denominations and for the most part there are only minor variations to distinguish them. One was the baptismal tank sunk into the floor in front of the pulpit in Baptist chapels, used in place of the local river which had been the scene of adult baptisms in early years.

The only major differences are between the buildings used by the Society of Friends and the rest. Their meeting-houses have no pulpit, and the area opposite the entrance was instead occupied by tiers of seats for the elders of the congregation. These, and much of the rest of the original seating of 1792, still survive largely intact at the North Walsham meeting-house.

Not only did chapels become more numerous in the late eighteenth and early nineteenth centuries, they also became more architecturally sophisticated, although Thomas Ivory's innovative Octagon Chapel in Norwich – built in 1756 by the Unitarians and 'perhaps the most elegant in all Europe' in the opinion of John Wesley – stands alone. The majority were still, for the most part, similar in style to contemporary houses. Thus they have symmetrical facades, often in soft red brick, with one or two doors; simple rectangular windows; and hipped pantile roofs.

Wortwell is a small village blessed with two particularly fine examples. The Baptist chapel, now owned by the Roman Catholic church, is an attractive red brick building of 1822. It has a hipped roof, is almost square in plan, and is entered through a single central doorway (the porch is modern). Inside, galleries run along the two sides and much of the original seating survives. At the other end of the village is the Independent meeting-house, built in 1773, again with a facade of red brick (although now painted cream). Today there is a single entrance doorway, but closer inspection reveals that there were originally two, now converted to windows: this is a good example of how these buildings, although of no very great antiquity, can have quite complex building histories and need to be examined with some care.

Towards the end of the period under discussion more architectural sophistication becomes evident, especially in the towns: at Little Walsingham, for example, in the Methodist chapel of 1793, with its round-arched windows, pedimented porch – and fine weather vane. Other urban chapels have different fashionable touches, like the pointed windows which bring a little gentleman's gothick to East Dereham's Congregational church of c.1815. Such embellishments, and in particular the adoption of classical features, were to be an increasingly important feature of chapel architecture in the decades after 1820.

The Octagon, Colegate, Norwich. Built by the Unitarians in 1756 to replace an earlier chapel, this must surely be the most distinctive and sophisticated eighteenth-century meeting-house in Norfolk. Designed by the prestigious Norwich architect Thomas Ivory, it was later described by John Wesley as 'perhaps the most elegant in all Europe'.

Wortwell in south Norfolk is blessed with two particularly fine nonconformist chapels. The earliest, the Independent meeting-house, was built in 1773. The cream paint obscures a facade of red brick, but a more important alteration can be detected in the cracks in the brickwork beneath the windows which show that the structure – like many early chapels – originally had two doors.

Wortwell Baptist chapel, now owned by the Roman Catholic church, was built in 1822. The red brick symmetrical facade and hipped roof are typical of the period. Inside, galleries run along the two sides of the building.

Congregational chapel, East Dereham. Erected around 1815, the pointed windows bring a touch of gentleman's gothick to this chapel, which was later downgraded to a school room after the construction of the new Cowper Memorial Church in 1874.

Classical Chapels: c.1820 – 1860.

From c.1820 until well into the second half of the nineteenth century most nonconformist chapels in Norfolk were built in a loosely classical style which harks back to the fashions of the previous century. Pilasters, string courses, pediments, fanlights and sash windows remained popular throughout the county. Dissenters had always built their chapels in styles which contrasted starkly with the medieval gothic of parish churches thus emphasising their difference and their separateness. Methodists may also have regarded an eighteenth-century style as reflecting that in which their founding forefathers built their first chapels. John Wesley himself laid down guiding principles regarding the proportions and measurements of suitable chapel buildings and his advice was followed for many years. All these factors played their part in encouraging a degree of architectural conservatism on the part of dissenting congregations.

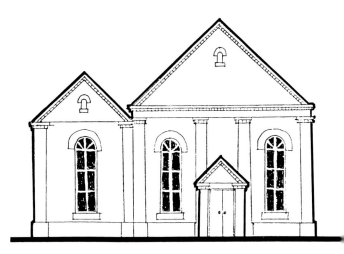

Hemsby, Primitive Methodist. Built of local white Somerleyton brick, the chapel of 1879 has its classical details highlighted in red brick. The neat Sunday school building next to the chapel carefully echoes its style (Drawing by F. Warns).

Besthorpe Primitive Methodist chapel, 1866.

The returns of the 1851 Census of Places of Religious Worship show that a very large number of chapels were built in the years between 1820 and the Census, particularly by the Methodists. Fieldwork by the recorders, however, has found that many of these were subsequently rebuilt, altered or extended. A total of 123 chapels built between 1820 and 1860 remain relatively unaltered and these show how style and design gradually changed and developed. The earliest show considerable continuity with those erected in the previous period. Fifty-four are simple buildings, either square or, more commonly, rectangular and with a hipped roof. There is usually a single doorway only and the pulpit is on the opposite short wall facing the entrance. Some have a pediment or pilasters, but architectural detailing is usually very restrained. Most have plain sash windows although there are three examples with round arched windows: the first indication of a popular style to come.

During the last twenty years of this period

ectangular chapels with gable roofs became increasingly the norm. This gable end was the main facade – the face the chapel presented to the world – and a good deal of money and effort were expended to give it smart detailing in good materials. It was at this time that builders began to use coloured bricks to highlight features such as windows, doorways, pediments and string courses. In contrast the sides and rear were usually of rather simple construction, an economical way of eking out precious building funds: 'Queen Anne at the front and Mary Ann at the back' aptly sums up most of the chapels built in this period. From the 1840s the simple building with a gable roof, door in the gable end, sash or round-arch windows and restrained detailing in a classical vein became almost universal until the appearance of gothic chapels at the end of the century.

Town chapels were usually larger and more stylish than country ones: they were more frequently designed by professional architects. At Downham Market the Free Methodist chapel has an imposing facade; at Kings' Lynn the Stepney Baptist chapel of 1841 has a pleasingly proportioned front while the Congregational church, now sadly demolished, had a striking classical elevation. Lady Lane Wesleyan chapel built in 1824 on what is now the Bethel Street car park in Norwich was also strongly classical in style with its pilasters, sash windows and symmetrical proportions.

Friends' Meeting-House, Goat Lane, Norwich. In 1679 a meeting-house was opened on this site: it was replaced in 1826. The heavy portico, pilasters and symmetrical flanking wings emphasise the classical influence in the design by J. Patience.

Methwold, Wesleyan Methodist. A classical brick facade of 1831 conceals the surprise of a flint rear wall with the round-headed windows so beloved of the later nineteenth century. The front of this building was imitated by both the Wesleyan Methodists in 1843 and the Primitive Methodists in 1871 at the nearby village of Northwold.

1860 Onwards

The Religious Census shows that by 1851 nonconformists were nearly as numerous as Anglicans in Norfolk, and from the 1860s the county witnessed a phenomenal burst of building activity to cope with larger or additional congregations. At first the design of chapels changed little. Most continued to be built in a broadly classical styles, although some urban chapels were erected in a somewhat flamboyant Italianate development of this like Chapelfield Road and Queen's Road Methodist chapels in Norwich. In the second half of the century, however, chapels in gothic style began to be built in increasing numbers.

Since the late eighteenth century there had been a revival of interest in gothic architecture, a style which had been largely ignored since the Reformation. It was first used for country houses and villa residences, but from the 1830s – under the influence of the Oxford Movement and the Ecclesiologists – gothic was increasingly employed for the new churches being erected in some numbers in the growing industrial towns. Numerous books of plans and details were published including, in 1850, one by a Wesleyan Methodist, F.J. Jobson. He argued that the gothic style was eminently suitable not only for Anglican churches, but also for nonconformist chapels, being both cheaper and more fitting for places of worship than the dominant classical style. He illustrated designs for gothic chapels and schoolrooms, both large and small, and during the second half of the century all nonconformist denominations were building some chapels in this mode.

The first example to be built in Norfolk seems to have been the Union Chapel in King's Lynn (now the Museum), designed by G.E.Street in 1859. From the outside a vast gothic pile like this could be mistaken for an Anglican church and the elaborate detailing is in sharp contrast to the somewhat simpler chapels of the eighteenth and early nineteenth centuries. In rural

Great Yarmouth Primitive Methodist Temple. A magnificent example of a late nineteenth-century Italianate chapel, sadly demolished in 1972.

areas, too, gothic began to take hold, as pointed, vaguely 'gothic' arches appeared instead of round-arched or rectangular openings for doors and windows. Most small rural chapels were, however, designed and built by local builders, men who were not always concerned with architectural purity. As a result a bizarre mixture of gothic and classical styles can sometimes be found in the same building. The Wesleyan chapel at Langley illustrates this tendency particularly well.

The small Methodist chapel at Langley illustrates how local builders sometimes used a random selection of architectural styles. Here a classical pediment is combined with pointed gothic windows and door on the main facade.

The Free Methodist chapel in Holt, built in 1862 to designs by Thomas Jeckyll, is one of the earliest gothic chapels in Norfolk.

The Primitive Methodist chapel at Postwick/ Thorpe St Andrew, built in 1901 (Drawing by M. Muir).

Dereham Road, Norwich, Baptist. A large panel of stonework rises out of the entrance pillars. It is engraved with stylised flowers. The central pillar is of red marble.

The Wesleyan chapel at Overstrand, designed by Edward Lutyens in 1898, is unique. The light in the chapel comes from the semicircular lunette windows below the roof, and the building has been officially 'listed' as an early example of this architect's work.

Nonconformist town chapels were often built to accommodate very large numbers. Chapelfield Road United Methodist chapel, Norwich, with wide galleries on three sides, can seat a substantial congregation. The organ and choir are placed in a special recess behind the pulpit: originally the pulpit was higher and even more imposing.

The years between 1890 and 1910 saw an increasing emphasis on gothic. Indeed, of the 106 surviving chapels built between 1890 and 1910, no less than fifty eight are in the gothic style. The others are in the traditional, simple, classical mould, with one notable exception: the Wesleyan Methodist chapel at Overstrand. This was designed at the request of Lord Battersea by Edward Lutyens, then at the start of his career. This unique structure, reminiscent of an overturned boat, is in striking contrast to other contemporary chapels.

Just as the external appearance of nonconformist chapels began to draw closer to that of Anglican churches in this period, so too did their internal layout. Although the high central pulpit still dominated the interior until the very end of the century, there was a new emphasis on music. Large organs were installed, often in a specially built extension behind the pulpit, together with accommodation for a choir. The position of the communion table also became more prominent, often now being placed in front of the pulpit, perhaps with rails around. In time, the pulpit was moved to one side, so that the table provided the central focus within the building.

Tunstead Wesleyan chapel, now converted to a barn, illustrates the style of many early nineteenth-century chapels. It was built on a small parcel of land allotted under the Enclosure Award of 1820, and is constructed of clay, with a hipped, pantile roof. It is a rare survival of this type of building since clay walls deteriorate rapidly if not maintained.

Mile Cross, Norwich, Methodist. An art-deco corbel of 1934 provides a stylish detail in this wide barrel-vaulted church.

Croxton Primitive Methodist chapel (1865) is typical of many small country chapels, especially those constructed by the Primitive Methodists. It is built of local flint with red brick quoins and window dressings.

New chapels continued to be built, albeit on a much reduced scale, throughout the twentieth century. Most were erected in the expanding suburbs of Norwich and the other major towns. Some are strictly utilitarian structures but others reflect the architectural fashions of their time. Notable examples include the Methodist church at Mile Cross in Norwich, with its fine art deco features; the 1930s Christian Science Church in Recorder Road, Norwich, a tall brick structure with narrow gothic windows of 1935; the very '1960s' Methodist church at Sheringham; the attractive octagonal extension made to Jessop Road United Reform Church in Norwich in 1969; and one of the newest, the Methodist church at Acle, built in 1989. Since World War II the emphasis has been on buildings which can be used for a whole range of different purposes throughout the week as well as for worship on Sundays, and which include facilities for the elderly, playgroups and youth clubs.

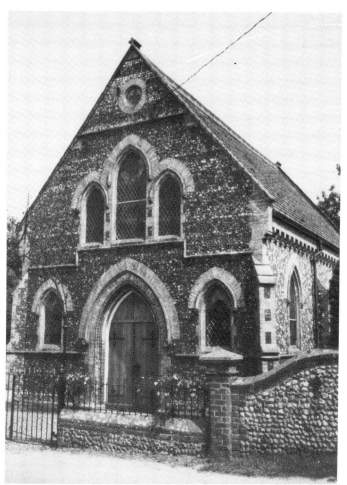

In 1895 the builders of Great Walsingham Wesleyan chapel used knapped flint with white brick dressings to give a more expensive and prestigious effect to their chapel.

Carstone is the local building stone of north west Norfolk and the Methodist New Connexion chapel of 1851 at Dersingham is one of a group of chapels in this area which use this material.

While travelling round the county the surveyors found that they could almost always spot the distinctive style of a chapel building even when drastically altered. Yet in spite of this apparent uniformity they also found that on closer inspection each building was different. Building materials often reflected local vernacular traditions; pebbles in north Norfolk, carr stone in the west, clay lump in the south of the county, brownish-red bricks in the Fens, and red and white bricks in the centre of the county. The early, somewhat 'domestic' meeting-houses and chapels had little architectural embellishment, but later buildings often had more complex detailing, each unique to a particular building. Though they are rarely architectural masterpieces, nonconformist chapels have been ignored for too long. Each one is different and almost all are worthy of our attention.

Hockwold, Primitive Methodist. Originally built for the Primitive Methodists about 1860, this chapel is now used as a doctor's surgery. Flint, brick and chalk can all be seen in its walls.

Converted or Demolished Chapels

As a nonconformist congregation grew, so resources were found to build a chapel: but over the years changes might occur which would render this building redundant. A poorly-built structure, a rapidly-growing congregation, a need for schoolroom accommodation, even the wish for something more fashionable or prestigious, could all prompt the decision to rebuild, leaving the trustees to decide whether to demolish or convert the original building.

If a new site was available, then the old property could be sold to help raise funds for the new, as happened in Upton. Frequently the old building was then converted to some new use. At Wendling this happened twice: the Primitive Methodists built a chapel in 1848 which was replaced in 1877; in 1914 this too was replaced by the present building. The first chapel was used for many years as a shed, the second is now an antique shop.

In 1824 the Baptists of Great Ellingham built a new chapel. The date stone reads 1699, commemorating the founding of the church in the village and illustrates how a date stone does not necessarily prove the age of a building.

Runham, Primitive Methodist chapel. The chapel of 1902 was built abutting the earlier small chapel of 1868. This was a regular arrangement with the older building finding uses as a Sunday school and meeting hall. Conversion to a house in 1988 retained the original features of the chapel.

More usually the existing chapel was either enlarged, as in the case of the Congregational chapel at Harleston, or a new chapel was built on the same plot. When this happened the previous building was sometimes retained for alternative use. At Loddon both the Primitive Methodists and the Wesleyan Methodists built new chapels in the 1890s, keeping the old buildings to serve as schoolrooms. At Kirby Cane the new chapel of 1892 was attached to the old, the latter being used to provide additional seating and a vestry. Rebuilding was constantly occurring throughout the nineteenth century and particularly in the period between 1860 and 1900. In recent years new chapels have been built to replace outmoded Victorian buildings unsuitable for the wide range of activities which now need to be catered for. Typical of this trend is the new chapel opened at Acle in 1989 which rendered the building of 1883 obsolete. Not all congregations prospered and over the years many

chapels have closed leaving the redundant buildings to decay, be demolished or to be sold for conversion.

The union of the Methodist churches in 1932 meant that in villages with both Primitive Methodist and Wesleyan chapels only one building was needed and often the redundant building survives converted to another use. More recently congregations have declined and with increasing mobility it makes sense for several small congregations to amalgamate in one centre. Changes in the distribution of population have also had an effect. In Norwich, King's Lynn and Great Yarmouth new buildings serve new suburbs such as the Bowthorpe Road and Heartsease Lane Methodist churches in Norwich, while at the new estates at Bowthorpe and Thorpe Marriott on the outskirts of the city ecumenical churches have been built. In the town centres many chapels have been demolished or have found new uses. Among those which have disappeared are several of great importance to the history of nonconformity in Norwich: the Methodist chapels in

Timberhill, Norwich, Baptist. Originally a warehouse, this building was converted to a chapel in 1832. It is no longer used for religious purposes and is being advertised for commercial use once again.

Calvert Street (opened in 1811) and Lady Lane (built in 1824) as well as the Tabernacle in Bishopgate and Chapelfield Congregational Church have all disappeared since 1930. At King's Lynn the Congregational chapel and the original Quaker meeting-house have gone, while in Yarmouth several chapels were destroyed by wartime bombing and others have been demolished since, including Park Baptist chapel in 1990.

Redundant chapels have been put to all manner of uses: the survey recorded examples converted to barns, stores, a doctor's surgery, a theatre scenery workshop, an undertaker's shop, an antique shop, an estate agent's office, and a public library, but the most common conversions are to houses. With sympathetic handling conversion can be successful and still retain features which indicate the building's previous use; a good conversion means that the building remains as witness to an important aspect of social history.

Reepham Baptist chapel. The present 'Companion Cottages' disguise a Baptist chapel erected in 1827. The building was sold to the Wesleyan Reformers in 1850 for use as a hall and has now been converted to houses.

Kenninghall, Baptist. The Particular Baptist chapel of 1807 is now a pottery yet retains its original character.

Wells, Wesleyan Methodist. Originally a public house, this building was transformed into a chapel in 1808. Now its is used as a public library.

Swanton Abbot, Primitive Methodist. The house of God now in the service of the god of the road.

Great Witchingham, Primitive Methodist. This little gothic gem built in 1905 and now converted to a house is more elaborate than the usual country chapel and must have cost much more. That the Primitive Methodists in central Norfolk were ready to erect such an elaborate chapel attests the extent of their confidence at this time.

Tin Tabernacles

Improved technology in timber and steel construction, together with improved methods of mass production, meant that by the end of the nineteenth century manufacturers were able to supply and erect complete buildings at low cost, ready for worship within a couple of weeks. These chapels had a timber frame which supported a cladding of corrugated iron or wood and were decorated with such 'churchy' features as diminutive spires, pointed windows and doors. They were usually provided with internal fittings in a vaguely medieval mode.

Wood Dalling, Salvation Army. This wooden chapel stands isolated beyond the edge of the village. Constructed at the beginning of the twentieth century by the firm of Boulton and Paul, it is now used as a shed.

Smallburgh Baptist chapel. The Sunday school to the rear of the chapel is housed in a 'tin tabernacle', said to have served formally as a chapel elsewhere.

Most of the 'tin tabernacles' erected in Norfolk were supplied by the renowned Norwich engineering firm of Boulton and Paul. According to their 1902 catalogue, they could construct on the purchaser's site a gothic-style church for £580 or a simple Mission Room measuring forty feet by twenty for £210. Some of these buildings are still in use today. Many more have not survived, not so much because they are prone to decay, but because they did not meet the requirements of later congregations.

The Educational and Social Role of the Chapel

The later eighteenth and nineteenth centuries saw increasing concern about the conditions of the poor and particularly those of poor children. Improvement in working conditions for children coincided with increasing educational opportunities provided by the National Schools, supported by the parish churches and after 1808 by the day schools set up by the nonconformist British and Foreign School Society. At the same time there was a rapid growth in the Sunday school movement and while the Anglican Church played its part, in many towns and villages it was the chapel Sunday school which provided the only formal education for many children until the Education Act of 1870. Even after 1870, when all children were legally required to attend day school, Sunday schools continued to flourish, drawing in large crowds of children of all ages.

Each chapel day or Sunday school was independently established by a local body or individual and run by members of the congregation, though the various denominations also set up agencies to help with support and with the supply of books. Children, and some adults, were taught basic reading, writing and Biblical studies. The teachers were drawn from all social backgrounds, many from the working class, and students often progressed to become teachers.

At first, classes were held wherever a suitable room could be found, but increasingly special schoolrooms were provided. Occasionally, as we have seen, when a new chapel was built the old building became a Sunday school. This happened in the case of Fakenham Primitive Methodist chapel and the Wesleyan chapel at Reepham, to give but two examples. More usually the school was a purpose-built structure, either free-standing or attached to the rear or side of the chapel. Some of those erected in the towns were very large buildings capable of accommodating hundreds

North Walsham, Quaker Meeting-House. The Society of Friends has always been assiduous in preserving its documents in its meeting-houses. It has also been keen to provide a library for members.

Sunday school certificate. Scripture examinations were taken annually by large numbers of Sunday school scholars. The art nouveau decoration here is similar to that on many of the certificates awarded in the early twentieth century.

of students. In 1891 the United Methodist chapel in Crooks Place, Norwich (the forerunner of Chapelfield Road chapel) had no less than 1153 scholars on its Sunday school roll. But many village chapels also provided surprisingly large school rooms. Terrington St Clement Methodist chapel built a Sunday school in 1885 to accommodate 300 children. Ten years later a new class was added and in 1922 three more rooms

Newton St Faith, Primitive Methodist. Sunday school outings were eagerly awaited. This group, photographed in 1913, are just setting out for a day by the sea at Cromer.

were built. This continuing expansion was typical, and by the 1860s even the smallest village chapel usually had a small schoolroom, often with a fireplace or iron stove. Sunday school places were not restricted to the children of chapel-goers and in the years before the 1870 Education Act many parents took advantage of the chance for their children to receive some basic schooling. Occasionally a day school was attached to the chapel, as at North Lopham and at Boughton.

During the nineteenth century chapels were also important in the social life of Norfolk's towns and villages. Special sermons, lectures, concerts, harvest suppers and tea meetings were arranged, often a

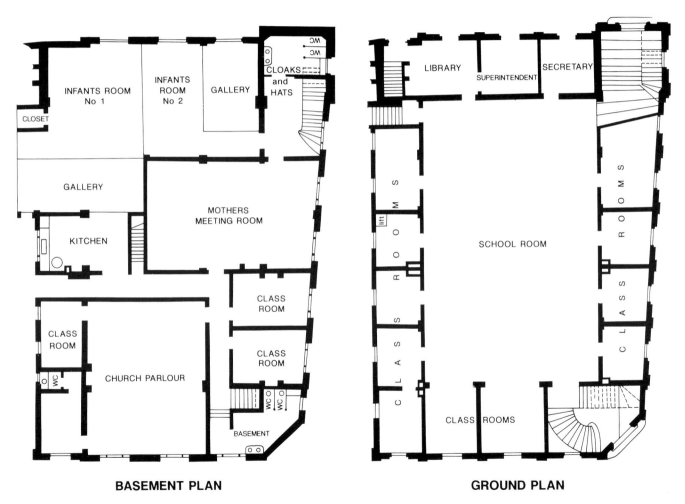

BASEMENT PLAN

GROUND PLAN

Princes Street Congregational, Norwich. Plans of the basement, ground and first floors in 1879, showing the formidable provision of rooms and facilities.

fund-raising events, and the Chapel anniversary, Sunday school anniversary and Sunday school outing were highlights of the year. Local newspapers are full of accounts of such events; the Norfolk News of 30 November 1872, for example, reported on a Public Meeting in aid of the fund for building the Cowper Memorial chapel at Dereham – 'a liberal and substantial tea with the usual accompaniments was excellently served'. Throughout the summer there are reports of Sunday school outings – with much emphasis placed on the teas provided!

In some places the chapel played a particularly central role in community life. The hamlet of Meeting Hill at Worstead consists of a small group of buildings clustered around the great Baptist chapel. This was built in 1829 to replace an earlier building founded in 1717 on a nearby site (both graveyards still survive). In 1820 Samuel Chapman of Norwich built six alms-houses just down the road for 'twelve poor persons . . . generally members of the Baptist congregation at Worstead . . .', and by 1844 there was a British School here which was also closely connected with the chapel. The hamlet also contains houses for the Minister, the Schoolmaster and the chapel caretaker, as well as a large stable for about forty horses belonging to visiting members of the congregation.

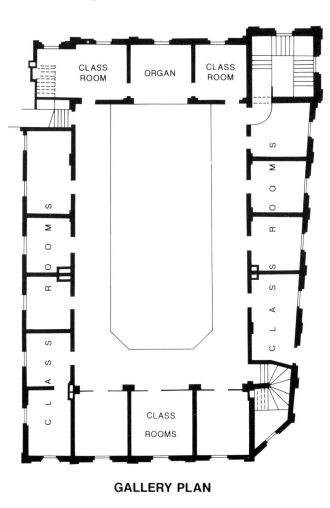

GALLERY PLAN

Scott Memorial Methodist church, Norwich. The chapel was opened in 1902, and was designed by A.F.Scott as a memorial to his father Jonathan Scott, a Methodist minister. A large and flourishing congregation was involved in a host of activities and produced its own magazine.

Caretaker's House, Meeting Hill. This pleasant building faces the chapel and is adjacent to the Minister's house.

Almshouses, Meeting Hill. Built in 1820 by Samuel Chapman for poor members of the congregation, the almshouses were supported by rents from land at Hellesdon.

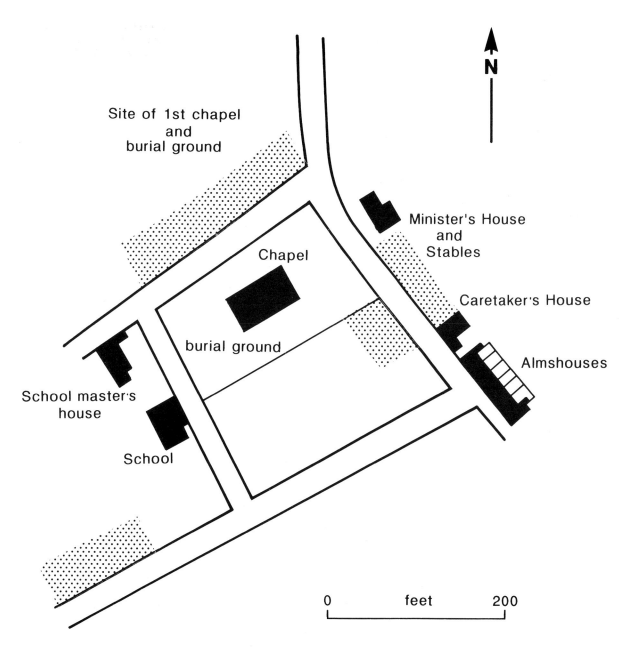

N

Site of 1st chapel
and
burial ground

Chapel

burial ground

Minister's House
and
Stables

Caretaker's House

Almshouses

School master's
house

School

0   feet   200

Meeting Hill, Worstead. A unique collection of buildings grew up around the Baptist chapel, including almshouses, stables, a school, and houses for minster, schoolmaster and caretaker.

Shipfield, Primitive Methodist. Harvest teas, suppers and auctions were high points in the social as well as the religious life of the chapel.

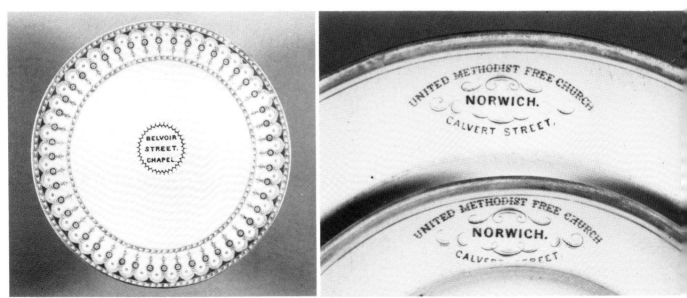

It was not uncommon for a special set of crockery to be ordered for use at social functions, decorated with the name of the chapel.

Burial Grounds

Some meeting-houses and chapels, and almost all of those established before 1800, have their own burial grounds. Usually these are attached to the chapel. Less frequently they occupy a separate plot located some distance away: at North Walsham the Friends' burial ground is nearly quarter of a mile down the road from their meeting-house. Even when side by side, however, chapel and burial ground did not always come into existence at the same time. At Attleborough, for example, the Baptist meeting-house (recently rebuilt) was erected in 1832, but land for the adjacent burial ground was only acquired in 1856.

Dissenting burial grounds are worth a close look. Many are peaceful, quiet places, like that beside the Friends' meeting house in Wells, or that at the Baptist chapel in Neatishead. They often contain fine examples of the eighteenth-century sculptor's art: indeed, it is striking that their stones are often as elaborately carved as any in a parish churchyard and are indistinguishable from them, for the most part, in terms of their iconography, design or inscription. They pass through the same fashions with (for example) cherubs giving way in the 1790s to urns as the main decorative motif. Only the burial grounds of the Society of Friends buck the trend with stones that usually bear no more than a simple inscription recording the name and details of the interred individual.

Some chapels have particularly good collections of stones, especially those of the Unitarians, Independents and Baptists, an indication, perhaps, of the kind of affluent middle-class congregations these

Wortwell Independent chapel. Contrary to what might be expected, gravestones in nonconformist burial grounds (with the exception of those erected by the Society of Friends) appear no different from those erected in neighbouring parish churchyards. The urn motif is typical of the early nineteenth century.

Kenninghall Baptist chapel. A striking row of nineteenth-century chest tombs.

denominations could attract in the eighteenth and early nineteenth centuries. Hapton has some fine early nineteenth-century examples, while the Independent chapel at Wortwell has a number dating back to its foundation in 1773. A fine chest tomb to the right of the path leading to the door bears the inscription:

> *In memory of James Whiting Gent. who erected this place of worship and purchased one at Harleston and settled a handsome endowment on them. He died 28th April 1785.*

Local mercantile and gentry patrons are often as well represented in the burial ground as manorial lords in a parish graveyard. Thus the burial ground of the Friends' Guildencroft meeting-house has large numbers of tombs of the Gurney family.

Unfortunately, Dissenting burial grounds have often suffered the same fate as Anglican ones: the stones cleared away to make way for the lawnmower, laid as paths or stacked up in piles by the chapel wall. And where chapels have been converted to new uses, the effect on the burial ground is usually disastrous.

Chapels and meeting-houses have played a very important role in the lives of Norfolk people over the last three hundred years. They are a vital part of the county's heritage and deserve more attention and more care than they have generally received. We hope that this small book will go some way towards raising public awareness of these buildings and the impact which they make upon the Norfolk landscape.

Neatishead Baptist chapel: a typical headstone of the late nineteenth century. The broken flower, symbolising mortality, was a favourite decoration.

Wortwell Independent chapel: the burial ground. The large chest tombs and numerous eighteenth– and early nineteenth-century headstones attest the prosperous, middle-class nature of the congregation.

GAZETTEER

This gazetteer contains very brief details of all the chapels identified by the recorders between 1988 and 1993. We have not dealt with the many buildings in the county which have been completely demolished, although we have included many which have been quite drastically converted to new uses.

The denomination given is that of the congregation which built the chapel or meeting-house and the present user is not given if it is the direct successor, such as a Wesleyan chapel now used by the Methodists or an Independent/Congregational chapel now used by the United Reformed Church. In the case of conversions, the new use given is that which pertained at the time when the building was surveyed.

The details given are:

Name of Parish

Denomination at time of building and any subsequent change

Date of existing building and of any alteration if known

Name of architect if known

The abbreviations used are:

U = used

X = unused

C = converted

* = Documentary evidence of earlier building or congregation.

The Primitive Methodist chapel at Aldborough was built on a side road in 1907. It replaced a very small and simple building beside the Green. As congregations expanded it was common for new, more prestigious chapels to be built.

ACLE – Wesleyan 1866, architect J.T.Bottle of Yarmouth, C store, *. **Primitive Methodist** 1883, X. **Methodist** 1989, U.

ALDBOROUGH – Primitive Methodist 1. 1844, C house. 2. 1907, U, *. **Plymouth Brethren** c1980, replaced earlier building, U, *.

ANMER – Methodist 1904, U.

ASHILL – Primitive Methodist 1893, U.

ASLACTON – Wesleyan 1834, war damage, rebuilt 1948, C house.

ATTLEBOROUGH – Baptist 1979, on site of earlier chapel, U, *. **Primitive Methodist** 1913, architect A.F.Scott, U, *. **Open Brethren** 1973, U.

AYLMERTON – Free Methodist 1887, C house.

AYLSHAM – Baptist 1791, extended 1876, 1904, 1984, U. **Wesleyan** 1842, new facade 1910, architect A.F.Scott, schoolroom 1895, extended 1975, 1980, U *. **Primitive Methodist** 1887, C Masonic Hall, *. **Wesleyan Reform** 1868, addition 1910, U, *. **Gospel Hall/Free Church** 1891, architect G.J.Skipper, Norwich, U.

BACONSTHORPE – Wesleyan 1844, C house.

BACTON – Baptist 1826, extended and school added, U.

BALE – Methodist n/k, C house.

BANHAM – Wesleyan n/k, C house, *. **Primitive Methodist** 1837, C farm store.

BANNINGHAM – Wesleyan Reform 1828, C store.

BARFORD – Primitive Methodist n/k, U, *.

BARNEY – Wesleyan 1844, converted from a cottage, X.

BARTON BENDISH – Wesleyan 1875, schoolroom 1891, C house, *.

BARTON TURF – Primitive Methodist registered as place of worship 1860, U, *.

BAWBURGH – Free Methodist 1866, U. (Formerly associated with Calvert Street), *.

BAWDESWELL – Wesleyan 1829, C house. **Primitive Methodist** 1866, C house, *. **Plymouth Brethren** 1903, X.

BEECHAMWELL/SHINGHAM – Wesleyan 1892, with schoolroom, X.

BEETLEY – Primitive Methodist 1876, school added 1894, U

BEIGHTON – Primitive Methodist 1862, with schoolroom, U.

BESTHORPE – Primitive Methodist 1866, U, *.

BILLINGFORD – Primitive Methodist 1908, C house, *.

Binham and Bodney are typical of countless small chapels built between 1860 and 1900 and indicate that only a proportion of congregations were attracted to gothic, the majority preferring a more classical style of building.

INHAM – **Primitive Methodist** 1868, U, *.

INTREE – **Primitive Methodist** 1877, U, (original aretaker's cottage adjoining).

LAKENEY – **Wesleyan/United Free** 1812, extended 846, schoolroom 1903, U, *. **Primitive Methodist/ alvation Army** 1850, C house.

LOFIELD HEATH – **Primitive Methodist** 1866, choolroom added, U.

ODHAM – **Free Methodist** 1866, U.

ODNEY – **Primitive Methodist** 1885, X.

OUGHTON – **Wesleyan** 1872, with schoolroom used as a day school until 1888), X, *.

OWTHORPE – **Ecumenical** 1986, U.

RADENHAM – **Primitive Methodist** 1877, C house.

RADFIELD – **Independent/Congregational** 1872 replaced chapel converted from a barn in 1697), C rm store, *.

RANCASTER – **Primitive Methodist** 1864, U, *.

RANCASTER STAITHE – **Primitive Methodist** 865, U.

RANDISTON – **Wesleyan Reform** 1956, X.

RESSINGHAM – **Wesleyan** n/k, C house, *. rimitive Methodist** 1900, architect Harvey inkworth, U, *.

RIDGEHAM – **Wesleyan** 1834, C village hall.

RININGHAM – **Gospel Hall** n/k, converted from a arn, U.

RINTON – **Wesleyan Reform/United Free** 1858, C ouse.

RISLEY – **Primitive Methodist** 1898, X, *.

RISTON – **Independent** 1775, with Manse added, . **Wesleyan** 1811, U. **Primitive Methodist** 1832, X. alvation Army** 1939, U, *. **Gospel Hall** n/k, U.

ROCKDISH – **Free Methodist** 1860, C workshop nd cottage, *.

ROOKE – **Baptist** 1839, restored 1932, 1990, U. rimitive Methodist** 1924, with new addition 1990, U.

BROOME – **Wesleyan** 1912, U.

BRUNDALL – **Mission Hall** 1993, replaced earlier building, U.

BUNWELL – **Primitive Methodist** 1876, C house, *.

BURGH NEXT AYLSHAM – **Primitive Methodist** 1868, C house, *.

BURGH ST PETER – **Wesleyan** c1835, enlarged later, C house and schoolroom, demolished 1979, *. **Primitive Methodist** 1864, C village hall.

BURNHAM MARKET – **Congregational/Methodist** 1807, altered 1878, C shop 1972. **Primitive Methodist** 1850, C house, *. **Salvation Army / Methodist** 1928, altered 1964, 1983, U by Methodists. **Open Brethren** n/k, converted from a cottage, U .

BURNHAM OVERY – **Primitive Methodist** 1860, C house.

BURNHAM THORPE – **Primitive Methodist** 1864, U, *.

BURNHAM ULPH and BURNHAM SUTTON – **Wesleyan** 1828, C house, *.

BURSTON – **Primitive Methodist** 1888, U by Fellowship for Evangelising Britain's Villages, *.

BUXTON HEATH – **Baptist** founded 1796, chapel demolished, schoolroom remains, X.

CAISTER – **Wesleyan** 1886, new hall 1980, U, *.

CARBROOKE – **Wesleyan** 1843?, C house. **Primitive Methodist** 1870, school 1896, X, *.

CARLTON RODE – **Baptist** 1812, school 1904, U.

CASTLE ACRE – **Baptist** 1841, new chapel adjacent 1872 (architect Mr Oakes of Swaffham), old chapel became schoolroom, C village hall. **Methodist (Primitive ?)** n/k , X.

CASTON – **Primitive Methodist** 1878, C house.

CATFIELD – **Primitive Methodist** 1836, school 1913, U.

Carleton Rode, Baptist. Built in 1812, this chapel stands alone on a minor road well outside the village. It is surrounded by a very extensive graveyard and nearby is a pit once used for the baptism of members.

CAWSTON – Wesleyan/Wesleyan Reform 1829, repaired 1866, school 1933, U, *. **Primitive Methodist** 1861, extended 1954, U, *.

CLAXTON – Baptist (Strict and Partic.) 1790 in place of earlier chapel, C house, * (destroyed by fire 1993).

CLENCHWARTON – Primitive Methodist 1881, hall added 1961, U.

CLEY – Wesleyan/United Free Methodist 1839, altered and enlarged 1866, C house. **Primitive Methodist** 1837 converted from a cottage, C house.

COLBY – Wesleyan 1846, extended 1891, C house. **Wesleyan Reform** 1905, U.

COLTISHALL – Wesleyan/Gospel Hall 1842, U. **Free Methodist/Methodist** 1878, altered 1970, U. **Exclusive Brethren** n/k, C shop. **Swedenborgian** used a room in a house.

CORPUSTY – Primitive Methodist 1859, U, *.

COSTESSEY – Baptist 1822, U. **Methodist** 1963, U, *.

CRANWORTH – Primitive Methodist 1865, schoolroom 1879, U, *.

CRIMPLESHAM – Free Church/United Methodist 1905, C village hall.

CROMER – Baptist (General)/Baptist (Independent) 1901, U. **Wesleyan/Methodist** 1910, (replaced earlier chapel), architect A.F.Scott, U, *. **Free Methodist** 1890, C library. **Gospel Hall** C20, U.

CROXTON – Primitive Methodist 1865, C store.

DENTON – Independent/Congregational 1821 on site of earlier chapel, restored 1963, U, *.

DENVER – Wesleyan 1864, X, *.

DEOPHAM GREEN – Primitive Methodist 1837, U.

DEREHAM – Independent/Congregational 1. c1815, C Scout hall. **2.** 1874, architect Edward Boardman, U, *. **Baptist 1.** 1784. **2.** New chapel 1859, old chapel converted to schoolroom, U. **Wesleyan/Methodist** 1880, architect Edward Boardman, U. **United Methodist** 1901, C shop. **Salvation Army** 1888, U. **Plymouth Brethren** 1938, U.

DEREHAM, ETLING GREEN – Congregational/Methodist 1880, U occasionally.

DEREHAM, TOFTWOOD – Methodist C20, U, *.

DERSINGHAM – Wesleyan 1890, architect J.A.Hillam of King's Lynn, U, *. **Methodist New Connexion** 1851, C house, *.

DICKLEBURGH – Baptist 1882, architect Rev. C. Stovell, U.

DILHAM – Primitive Methodist 1869, C part of house.

DISS – Independent/Congregational 1839, rebuilt, U, *. **Baptist** 1860 in place of older chapel, U, *. **Unitarian** 1822, C 1955 Masonic hall. **Society of Friends** 1744, school 1897, U. **Methodist** 1963, additions 1974, 1980, 1988, U, *. **Salvation Army** 1914, hall 1958, additions 1985, C shop. **Bethel Mission** n/k, U. **Christian Community** 1988, U. **Denmark St Hall** n/k, U.

DOWNHAM MARKET – **Society of Friends** 1701, C library. **Baptist (General)** 1800, C Masonic hall. **Wesleyan** 1810, altered 1830, 1864, 1876, schoolroom 1895, C amusement arcade. **Free Methodist** 1859, school 1865, vestry 1869, gallery 1897, C store. **United Methodist** 1965, U. **Salvation Army** 1882, U.

DOWNHAM MARKET, BARROWAY DROVE – **United Free Methodist** 1907, U, *.

DOWNHAM MARKET, SALTERS LODE – **Primitive Methodist** n/k, X.

DRAYTON – **Free Methodist** 1892, U.

EAST BARSHAM – **Primitive Methodist** 1887, X.

EAST HARLING – **Society of Friends** 1836, school 1903, X. **Primitive Methodist** 1865, school 1895, U, *.

EAST RUDHAM – **Wesleyan** 1824, C British Legion hall. **Primitive Methodist** 1862, X, *.

EAST RUNTON – **Primitive Methodist** 1896, architect A.F. Scott, U, *.

EAST RUSTON – **Methodist** 1928, U, *.

EAST WALTON – **Primitive Methodist** 1889, X.

EASTON – **Wesleyan** n/k, C house, *.

EDGEFIELD – **Primitive Methodist** 1883, C house, *. **Mission Hall** 1908, X.

Foulsham Baptist chapel, built in 1826 in the centre of the village.

EDINGTHORPE GREEN – Methodist 1880, C house.

ELSING – Primitive Methodist 1864, X, *.

EMNETH – Primitive Methodist 1864, 1911 new chapel alongside, architect T.M. Kerridge, U, *.

ERPINGHAM – Wesleyan Reform 1879, U, *.

FAKENHAM – Society of Friends founded in a barn, converted to meeting-house 1689, C. **Independent** 1819, C British Legion hall. **Baptist (Particular)** 1869, replaced chapel of 1808, U. **Congregational** 1895, school 1899, C antiques showroom. **Primitive Methodist** 1908, replaced chapel of 1825/1861 which became schoolroom, architect 1908 A.F.Scott, U, *. **Salvation Army** c1950 (on site of Wesleyan chapel bombed 1940), U.

FELTHORPE – Baptist 1831, U.

FELTWELL – Primitive Methodist n/k, C shop, *. **Methodist** 1935, U, *.

FERSFIELD – Primitive Methodist 1891, C house.

FIELD DALLING – Primitive Methodist 1871, C house, *. **Free Methodist** n/k, C house, *.

FINCHAM – Wesleyan 1862, C house, *. **Primitive Methodist** 1878, school added 1904, architect of school John Whitmore, X, *.

FLEGGBURGH – Wesleyan 1841, U.

FLITCHAM – Primitive Methodist 1885, X, *.

FORNCETT ST PETER, FORNCETT END – Calvinist/Baptist 1754, restored 1875, C grain store. **Primitive Methodist** 1865, U, *.

FORNCETT ST MARY – Primitive Methodist 1884, architect J. Kerridge, U.

FOULDEN – Wesleyan 1873, C garage store.

FOULSHAM – Baptist (Strict and Particular) 1826, original stables converted to rooms, U, *. **Primitive Methodist** 1871, X.

FOXLEY – Primitive Methodist 1898, U, *.

FRAMINGHAM EARL – United Methodist 1964 (replaced chapel 1878) extended, U, *.

FRAMINGHAM PIGOT – Baptist (Particular) 1808/9, C house.

FRANSHAM – Wesleyan 1877, X, *.

FREETHORPE – Primitive Methodist 1896, replaced earlier chapel, U, *.

FRETTENHAM – Methodist Free church 1929 replaced wooden chapel built c1855, U.

FULMODESTON – Primitive Methodist new facade 1902, U, *.

FUNDENHALL – Primitive Methodist 1890, C house.

GARBOLDISHAM – Primitive Methodist 1893, U, *.

GARVESTON – Primitive Methodist 1892, U, *.

GAYTON – Primitive Methodist 1870, extended 1883, U, *.

GAYTON THORPE – Primitive Methodist 1902, X.

GAYWOOD – Wesleyan 1874, U by Evangelical church, *.

GISSING – Wesleyan 1860, C house, *.

GOODERSTONE – Wesleyan 1895, U, *.

GREAT BIRCHAM – Primitive Methodist 1871, C house, *.

GREAT CRESSINGHAM – Methodist 1932, U, *.

GREAT DUNHAM – Primitive Methodist 1867, school 1888, U, *.

GREAT ELLINGHAM – Baptist 1824, U, *. **Wesleyan/Primitive Methodist 1843, U.**

GREAT FRANSHAM – Wesleyan 1877, X.

GREAT HOCKHAM – Primitive Methodist 1896, U, *.

GREAT MASSINGHAM – Wesleyan 1827, enlarged 1844, 1849, U. **Primitive Methodist** 1870, C garage, *. **United Methodist** 1853, C house.

GREAT MOULTON – Baptist 1890, prefabricated building, removed to Stowmarket Museum.

GREAT RYBURGH – Wesleyan 1845, altered 1883, blitzed 1942, reopened 1946, U. Architect of 1883 alterations E. Boardman. **Primitive Methodist** 1882, C house, *.

GREAT SNORING – Primitive Methodist 1874, U, *.

GREAT WALSINGHAM – Wesleyan 1895, U by Russian Orthodox Church, *.

GREAT YARMOUTH – Society of Friends 1694, enlarged 1807, U. **Congregational/United Reform** 1869, hall and school 1879, architect J. Bottle, C offices. **Congregational/Wesleyan** 1855, altered 1990, U. **Baptist (Strict)** 1874, U by Elim Pentecostal Church. **Baptist (Particular)** 1847, C school then warehouse. **Methodist** 1859, C shop. **Methodist** 1891, 1907 chapel converted to school, new chapel built, U. **Gospel Hall** 1960, U. **Emmanuel Hall** 1847, U.

GRESHAM (LOWER) – Primitive Methodist 1871, U.

GRESSENHALL – Primitive Methodist 1830, converted from a cottage, U.

GRIMSTON – Wesleyan 1873, architect A.J.Hillam, C photographic studio, *.

GRIMSTON, POTT ROW – Primitive Methodist, 1876, U.

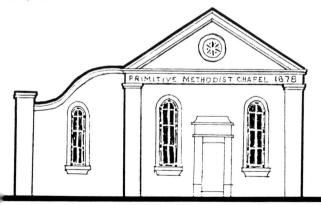

Halvergate, Primitive Methodist 1878. Plain pilasters and the use of bricks to outline the roof were an inexpensive way of giving a subtle classical flavour to many chapels built at this time (Drawing by F. Warns).

GUESTWICK – Independent 1695/1840, X.

GUNTHORPE – Wesleyan 1872, C.

HADDISCOE – Primitive Methodist 1872, X, *.

HALES – Primitive Methodist 1. 1840, C village hall. **2.** 1910, C house.

HALVERGATE – Primitive Methodist 1878, U, *.

HAPPISBURGH – Primitive Methodist 1862, C house, *.

HAPTON – Presbyterian/Unitarian 1749, C house.

HARDINGHAM – Primitive Methodist 1908, X.

HARLESTON – Congregational 1819, extended with new facade 1886, architect E.Boardman, school 1906, U. **Wesleyan** 1886, U, *.

HARPLEY – Primitive Methodist 1871, U, *.

HEACHAM – Wesleyan 1831, restored 1891, C furniture store. **Primitive Methodist** 1903, altered and new facade C20, U, *.

HELHOUGHTON – Primitive Methodist 1880, C house, *.

HELLESDON – Salvation Army 1938, new front and extensions 1989, U. **Non-denominational** 1974, U.

HEMPNALL – Wesleyan 1895, school 1906, U , *.

HEMPSTEAD – Wesleyan n/k, C house.

HEMSBY – Congregational/Evangelical Congregational 1862, U. **Primitive Methodist** 1879, U, *.

HETHERSETT – Baptist 1898, extended 1962, U. **Wesleyan 1.** 1817, now schoolroom, **2.** new chapel 1922, altered 1981, U.

HEVINGHAM – Free Methodist/Gospel Hall n/k, U.

HICKLING – Primitive Methodist 1882, school 1896, U, *.

HILGAY – Wesleyan 1871, school 1912, U, *. **Primitive Methodist** 1838, extended, C shop.

HILGAY, TEN MILE BANK – Primitive Methodist 1878, architect J. Kerridge, school added, X.

HINDOLVESTON – Wesleyan 1836, school 1954, U. **Primitive Methodist** n/k, C barn.

HINDRINGHAM – Wesleyan 1834, C builder's store. **Primitive Methodist** 1845, altered, U.

HINGHAM – Society of Friends 1707, C house. **Congregational** 1836, renovated and new facade 1898, architect A.F.Scott, U. **Primitive Methodist** 1900, U, *. **Methodist** n/k, C house.

HOCKERING – Primitive Methodist n/k, renovated 1897, X, *.

HOCKWOLD – Primitive Methodist n/k, C doctor's surgery, *. **Methodist** c1910, U, *.

HOLM-NEXT-THE-SEA – Primitive Methodist 1875, C house, *.

HOLME HALE – Wesleyan 1898, C house, *.

HOLT – Wesleyan 1. 1813, C houses and shop. **2.** 1838, restored 1893, C St John Ambulance hall. **Primitive Methodist** 1872, C offices, *. **Free Methodist/Methodist** 1862, architect Thomas Jeckyll U, *.

HORNINGTOFT – Primitive Methodist n/k, C garage.

HORSEY – Methodist 1958, U.

HORSFORD – Free Methodist 1862, U, *.

HORSHAM ST FAITH – Wesleyan 1822, U.

HUNSTANTON – Union (Baptist and Congregational) 1870, U. **Wesleyan** 1896, U, *. **Church of Christ Scientist** U.

Harpley, Primitive Methodist. Heavy dogtooth brickwork above the doorway of 1871 shows an imaginative yet ponderous use of the medium.

Hemsby Congregational chapel was built in 1862, an unusually late date for a new foundation by this denomination. Equally unusual is the burial ground attached, a feature more characteristic of early chapels and meeting-houses.

The Primitive Methodist chapel in London Road, King's Lynn was built in 1857 in a vaguely gothic, vaguely Italianate style.

Hindolveston, Wesleyan Methodist. The square chapel with its symmetrical facade, hipped roof and general eighteenth-century air lasted well into the middle of the succeeding century.

HUNWORTH – Primitive Methodist 1898, C house, *.

ITTERINGHAM – Primitive Methodist 1846, extended 1907, U. **Wesleyan Reform** 1861, C house.

KELLING – Primitive Methodist n/k, C house.

KENNINGHALL – Baptist (Particular) 1807, extended 1832, 1874, C pottery studio. **Wesleyan** 1854, rebuilt and enlarged 1873, C sports hall, *. **Primitive Methodist** 1853, C barn, *.

KETTLESTONE – Primitive Methodist n/k, closed 1870, C house.

KING'S LYNN – Society of Friends, Bridge St. converted from Public House, replaced meeting-house in New Conduit St demol. 1970, U. **Stepney Baptist** 1841, altered 1871–85, U by New Life Christian Fellowship. **Baptist, Saddlebow Rd,** 1900, architect J. Fenton, U. **Union Chapel, Independent Baptist and non denom.** 1859, architect G. Street, C museum. **Primitive Methodist, London Rd**, 1857, with additions, architect J.A.Hiller, U, *. **Wesleyan Reform/Methodist New Connexion**, Railway Rd, 1853, C garage. **Wesleyan Reform/Primitive Methodist, Highgate** 1883, U, *: **London Rd** n/k, C offices. **Brethren, London Rd** c1980, U. **Salvation Army, Wellesley St** 1981, replaced hall of 1879.

KIRBY CANE – Wesleyan 1841, enlarged 1892, school 1922, U.

KNAPTON – Primitive Methodist 1880 converted from barn, 1960 schoolroom, U.

LAKENHAM – United Reform C20, U.

LAMMAS – Society of Friends (and used by Methodists for a time) c1720, C house.

LANGHAM – Methodist 1935, C house.

LANGLEY – Wesleyan 1891, school 1935, C house, *.

ARLING – Wesleyan 1881 converted from barn, C, *.

LENWADE AND GREAT WITCHINGHAM – Wesleyan/Wesleyan Reform 1826, C house. **Primitive Methodist** 1905, C house, *. **Methodist** n/k, C house.

LESSINGHAM – Primitive Methodist 1891, U, *.

LETHERINGSETT – Primitive Methodist 1898, C house.

LIMPENHOE – Primitive Methodist 1877, U, *.

LINGWOOD – Primitive Methodist 1867, school 1868, altered 1975, U, *.

LITCHAM – Primitive Methodist 1867, X, *. **United Methodist** 1909, U.

The Wesleyan chapel in Long Stratton, still in use as the local Methodist church, illustrates the way a chapel can change over the years. It was built in 1830, enlarged in 1845, a gallery added in 1883 which was subsequently removed in 1889, and in 1989 the interior was completely refitted to provide the facilities required by a modern congregation.

LITTLE BARNINGHAM – Free Methodist 1860, X.

LITTLE CRESSINGHAM – Wesleyan n/k, X.

LITTLE SNORING – Primitive Methodist 1860, C house, *.

LITTLE WALSINGHAM – Independent/Free Methodist 1844, C house. **Wesleyan** 1793–4, school 1891, U.

LODDON – Wesleyan 1. 1835, converted to schoolroom. **2.** new chapel 1893, U, *. **Primitive Methodist 1.** 1852, converted to schoolroom. **2. new chapel** 1899, C youth centre.

LONGHAM – Free Methodist 1869, C house.

LONG STRATTON – Independent/Congregational 1840, new facade 1872, U. **Wesleyan** 1830, enlarged 1845, altered 1883, 1889, 1990, U.

LUDHAM – Wesleyan 1867, architect Mr Chaplin of Ludham, U, *. **Primitive Methodist** 1913, C house.

LYNG – Primitive Methodist 1857, U, *.

MARHAM – Primitive Methodist 1879, C store, *. **Methodist** 1904, X, *.

MARSHAM – Primitive Methodist 1881, U, *.

MARSHLAND ST JAMES – Primitive Methodist 1891, architect J.W.Crouch of Wisbech, school 1927, now the chapel, U.

MARTHAM – Baptist (strict) 1879, U, *. **Primitive Methodist 1.** 1844, C Oddfellows hall, **2.** 1881, U, *.

MATTISHALL – Society of Friends 1687, C store. **Independent/Congregational 1.** (at Old Moor) 1771, C store. **2.** (at Welgate) 1857, U, (originally lecture hall for Old Moor chapel). **Primitive Methodist – 1.** 1856, C garage, *. **2.** 1900, U.

METHWOLD – Wesleyan 1831, U, *.

METHWOLD HYTHE – Wesleyan n/k, C house.

MIDDLETON, BLACKBOROUGH END – Wesleyan (or Mission Room) n/k, C business premises. **FAIR GREEN Methodist** 1903, C storeroom, *. **Mission Hall** 1894, X.

Martham Primitive Methodist chapel, built in 1881, retains the traditional arrangement with central pulpit, organ behind, communion table in front and texts painted on the wall.

MILEHAM – Wesleyan 1849, C store. **Primitive Methodist/Gospel Hall** 1886, X, *.

MORLEY ST BOTOLPH – Primitive Methodist 1905, U.

MULBARTON – Primitive Methodist 1900, U.

MUNDESLEY – Non-denominational founded 1843, altered, school added 1892. U. **Wesleyan** 1897, architect Eade and Johns, Ispwich U, *.

MUNDFORD – Wesleyan 1873, U.

MUNDHAM – Methodist 1899, C art studio, *.

NARBOROUGH – Wesleyan 1871, U, *.

NEATISHAEAD – Baptist 1811, U, *.

NECTON – Baptist founded 1802, repaired and improved 1882, U, *. **Wesleyan** n/k, C house.

NEW BUCKENHAM – Wesleyan 1884, U, *. **Primitive Methodist** 1879, C house, *.

NEWTON ST FAITH – Wesleyan/Primitive Methodist 1821, C garage.

NORDELPH (UPWELL Parish) – Wesleyan 1861, C house, *.

NORTH CREAKE – Primitive Methodist 1876, school 1880, C house, *.

NORTH ELMHAM – Congregational 1824, C house **Primitive Methodist 1.** 1876, altered 1958, U. **2. (At BROOM GREEN)** n/k, X.

NORTH LOPHAM – Wesleyan 1810, school 1835, U, *. **Primitive Methodist** – C house, *.

NORTH PICKENHAM – Primitive Methodist 1912, X.

NORTH TUDDENHAM – Primitive Methodist 183?, C house.

NORTH WALSHAM – Society of Friends 1792, U. **Independent/Congregational** 1857 to replace chape of 1808, U by Evangelical Church, *. **Wesleyan 1.** 1820, C printing works, *. **2.** 1890, additions 1938 1987, U, *. **Primitive Methodist** 1873, C shop.

Salvation Army 1899, U. **Gospel Hall** converted from a barn.

NORTHWOLD – Wesleyan 1843, C store. **Primitive Methodist** 1871, school 1906, C store, *.

NORTON SUBCOURSE – Primitive Methodist rebuilt 1900, U, *.

NORWICH – Independent/Congregational – Old Meeting, Colegate, 1693 school 1842, U. **Congregational/United Reform – Princes Street** 1819, enlarged 1869, school 1879–80, architect Edward Boardman, U.

United Reform – Jessop Road 1930/1969, U. (* successor to Chapelfield Congregational church built 1858, school 1907, destroyed by bombing, school building survives C to other use.) **Ipswich Road** – 1954, extended 1992, with additions, U. **Lakenham** – 1920, now U by Norwich Christian Fellowship. **Trinity Church, Unthank Road** 1956 architect Bernard Feilden, on site of Baptist church destroyed by bombing, U.

Presbyterian/Unitarian – Octagon, Colegate 1756, founded 1672, present building replaces earlier chapel, U, *.

Baptist – St Mary's, Duke Street (Particular) 1952, U,*. On site of first chapel 1743, second chapel 1812, enlarged 1886, destroyed by bombing 1942. **Timberhill, (Strict and Particular)** 1832, C shop/store.

Colegate (General) 1814, C timber store.

Zoar, St Mary's Plain 1886, U.

Dereham Road 1905, architect A.F.Scott, U.

Silver Road (General) 1910, U.

Mile Cross built as Sunday school run from St Mary's 1937, altered to chapel 1987, U.

Witard Road, Heartsease 1959, U.

Society of Friends – Upper Goat Lane 1826, architect J.Patience, on site of earlier meeting-house, U, *.

Gildencroft 1698, bombed 1942, repaired 1958, C Day Centre.

The Old Meeting, Colegate, Norwich: detail of the sundial on the main facade before the date was changed from Arabic to Roman numerals (Photo RCHME Crown Copyright).

Puritan Austerity? The sumptuous decoration on a capital of the Old Meeting, Colegate.

Chapelfield Road, Norwich, United Methodist. Glazed tiles in brown and yellow form a frieze round the church.

Chapelfield Road, Norwich, United Methodist. Ironwork from the front of the gallery: no expense was spared to decorate this large city centre chapel in 1880.

Octagon Chapel, Norwich, Unitarian. Intricate ironwork at the apex of the octagonal roof hides the ventilation shaft.

Methodist – Wensum Chapel, Cowgate, (Primitive) 1842, U by Christian Evangelical Fellowship.

Queens Road (Primitive) 1873, C offices, *.

Nelson Street (Primitive) 1878, C.

Chapelfield Road (United) 1881, school and halls 1954, U.

Park Lane (Wesleyan) 1939, replaced chapel built 1895, U.

Thorpe Road (Primitive) 1902, architect A.F.Scott, C offices.

Heartsease Lane 1953, architect C.Dann, school 1961, replaced small chapel on Plumstead Rd destroyed by bombing, U, *.

Mile Cross 1933, architect Cecil Yelf, U.

Rosebery Road, Catton (Wesleyan/United Free) 1908, U.

Bowthorpe Road 1946/1973, architect C. Dann, successor to Dereham Road Primitive Methodist chapel, destroyed by bombing, U, *.

Salvation Army – Citadel, St Giles 1882, U. **Bull Close** c1890, U.

Swedenborgian – Park Lane 1890, U as Haymarket Meeting Rooms.

Railway Mission (non-denominational) – Prince of Wales Road 1885, U by Evangelical Free Church.

Free Church – Surrey Chapel 1976 replaced 1854 chapel in Surrey St, U, *.

Independent Evangelical – Ramsey Close 1959, U.

Douro Place converted from C of E Church Hall c1977, U.

Gospel Hall – Grapes Hill/Dereham Road n/k, C offices.

Church of Christ Scientist – Recorder Road 1934, architect H.G.Ibberson, U.

inces Street, Norwich, Congregational. Griffins snarl from the corners of this capital ich has a cherub at its centre. This rich facade of yellow brick was added in 1869 to ⁓ original chapel of 1819.

Chapelfield Road, Norwich, United Methodist. This detail of the main door shows the care bestowed on the architectural embellishment of a rich city chapel (Drawing by I. Muir).

OLD BUCKENHAM – Baptist 1831, altered 1857, school 1881, U. **Primitive Methodist** 1851, U, *

OLD CATTON – Baptist (Strict and Particular)/Primitive Methodist 1830, changed from Baptist to Primitive Methodist c1880, C funeral parlour.

ORMESBY ST MARGARET – Baptist 1836, U as Baptist church hall. **Wesleyan/Baptist** 1863, U by Baptists, *. **Primitive Methodist** 1894, C house.

OULTON – Congregational 1728, X but fittings remain. **Wesleyan Reform** 1911, U, *.

OUTWELL – Methodist 1962, U, *. **Salvation Army** 1883, X. (N.B. There are other chapels in Outwell but they are in Cambridgeshire).

OVERSTRAND – Wesleyan 1898, architect Edward Lutyens, U.

OVINGTON – Primitive Methodist n/k, X.

PENTNEY – Wesleyan 1882, C garage, *.

POSTWICK/THORPE ST ANDREW – Primitive Methodist 1901, U, *.

POTTER HEIGHAM – Methodist c1970, U, *.

PULHAM MARKET – Wesleyan 1863, school added, U, *.

PULHAM ST MARY – Particular Baptist 1843, C engineering workshop.

REEDHAM – Primitive Methodist 1881, U, *.

REEPHAM/HACKFORD – Baptist/Wesleyan Reform 1827, C house. **Wesleyan** 1816 with additions, U, *. **Primitive Methodist** 1845/7, C hall. **Salvation Army** n/k, C shop.

REPPS WITH BASTWICK – Primitive Methodist 1907, U, *.

RINGLAND – Wesleyan 1852, U.

RINGSTEAD – Primitive Methodist 1867, school 1922, X.

ROCKLAND ST PETER – Primitive Methodist 1859, U, *.

ROLLESBY – Primitive Methodist 1866, U, *.

ROUGHAM – Primitive Methodist 1877, U.

ROUGHTON – Primitive Methodist n/k, C house, *.

RUNCTON HOLME – Primitive Methodist n/k, C house.

RUNHALL – Primitive Methodist 1912, C house, *.

RUNHAM – Primitive Methodist 1868, C schoolroom, new chapel 1902, C house 1988.

SAHAM TONEY – Primitive Methodist 1876, U, *. **Free Methodist** n/k, C paint shop

SALHOUSE – Baptist (Strict and Particular) 1802, U. **Baptist** 1846, C house. **Methodist** 1967 successor to earlier Wesleyan Methodist chapel, U.

SALTHOUSE – Free Methodist 1891, C house, *.

SAXLINGHAM NETHERGATE – Undenominational 1890, U.

Reedham Primitive Methodist Chapel 1881 (painting by F. Warns

SAXLINGHAM THORPE – **Baptist** n/k, C house, *.

SCARNING – **Congregational/URC** 1884, U.

SCOULTON – **Primitive Methodist** 1909, C house, *.

SCRATBY – **Primitive Methodist** 1894, U, *.

SCULTHORPE – **Primitive Methodist** 1888, U.

SEA PALLING – **Baptist** 1860, C house. **Primitive Methodist** 1877, U, *.

SEDGEFORD – **Wesleyan** 1830, U, *. Primitive Methodist 1861, C house.

SHARRINGTON – **Wesleyan** 1866, C house.

SHELFANGER – **Baptist** 1821, C house, *. Wesleyan 1845, U.

SHERINGHAM – **Baptist** 1952, hall added 1974/5, U. **Free Methodist** 1850, C house. **Methodist** 1968, additions 1980, U, *. **Salvation Army** 1896, U. **Society of Friends** 1963, U, *. **Church of Christ Scientist**, U.

SHIPDHAM – **Congregational** 1881, U, *. **Wesleyan/United Methodist** 1900, X, *. **Primitive Methodist/Undenominational** 1861, U, *.

SHOTESHAM – **Free Methodist** 1879, school 1951, U.

SHOULDHAM – **Wesleyan** 1816, C house. **Primitive Methodist** n/k, C house.

SHOULDHAM THORPE – **Primitive Methodist** n/k, house.

SHROPHAM – **Primitive Methodist** 1884, C house, *.

SKEYTON – **Wesleyan** n/k, C house. **Wesleyan Reform** c1850, C house.

SLOLEY – **Primitive Methodist** 1869, U, *.

SMALLBURGH – **Baptist/Primitive Methodist** 1680, altered, schoolroom formerly a chapel moved from another site, U. **Wesleyan Reform** c1870, school 1939, U, *.

SNETTISHAM – **Wesleyan** 1908, U, *. **Primitive Methodist** n/k, C Guide hall, *. **Salvation Army** (built as Wesleyan chapel) n/k, U.

SOUTH CREAKE – **Independent** 1783, school 1894, X. **Primitive Methodist** 1883, C house, *.

SOUTH LOPHAM – **Baptist** n/k, U by Christian Brethren.

SOUTHERY – **Baptist (Strict)** 1847, U.

SOUTHREPPS – **Wesleyan** 1845, C house, *. **Primitive Methodist** 1864, U, *.

SOUTH WALSHAM, PILSON GREEN – **Primitive Methodist** 1869, C house.

SOUTH WOOTTON – **Primitive Methodist** 1875, U.

SPARHAM – **Primitive Methodist** 1864, C house, *. **Free Methodist** n/k, C nursery school.

SPIXWORTH – **Methodist** c1930, C chapel hall 1980 when new chapel built adjacent, U.

SPORLE – **Primitive Methodist** 1862, U, *.

SPROWSTON – **Methodist** 1958 successor to Shipfield Methodist Church, U, *. **Christian Fellowship** 1982, U.

STALHAM – **Baptist (Particular)** 1884, U, *.

STALHAM GREEN – **Methodist** n/k, U, *.

STANHOE – **Wesleyan** 1827, C house. **Primitive Methodist 1.** 1851, x, replaced by: **2.** 1892, U.

STIBBARD – **Wesleyan** 1910, U, *.

STIFFKEY – **Primitive Methodist** 1900, C antiques shop, *.

STOKE FERRY – **Wesleyan** 1903 with school, C house, *. **United Free** 1860, C garage.

STOKE HOLY CROSS – **Free Church** 1960, U.

STOKESBY – **Primitive Methodist 1.** n/k, closed 1907, C house. **2.** 1907, architect A.F.Scott, U, *.

STOW BARDOLPH, STOWBRIDGE – **Baptist (General)** 1825, X. **United Free Methodist** 1860, U.

STOW BEDON – **Primitive Methodist** n/k, C store, *.

Stibbard, Wesleyan Methodist. Each window is decorated with a different device yet the overall effect is of a unified design (1910).

SURLINGHAM – Wesleyan 1803, originally a barn, C house 1982.

SUSTEAD – Primitive Methodist 1889, vestry 1913, U.

SUTTON – Primitive Methodist 1. 1846, C house. **2.** 1899, replaced 1846 chapel, U, *.

SWAFFHAM – Baptist 1860, U, *. **Wesleyan** 1813, altered 1875, U.

SWANTON ABBOTT – Wesleyan 1829, C garage. **Wesleyan Reform** 1851, altered c1910, U. **Swedenborgian** room in a house in use c1890.

SWANTON MORLEY – Primitive Methodist 1868, U, *. **Free Church/C of E** C20, U.

SWANTON NOVERS – United Free Methodist n/k, C house.

SWARDESTON – Baptist n/k, C garage.

SYDERSTONE – Wesleyan 1862, X, *. **Primitive Methodist** 1887, U until 1993, *.

TASBURGH – Society of Friends 1707, altered 1773 C house. **Primitive Methodist** n/k, C office, *.

TAVERHAM, THORPE MARRIOTT – Methodist/C of E 1991, U.

TERRINGTON ST CLEMENT – Wesleyan 1844, school 1881, U. **Primitive Methodist** n/k, C house, * **Salvation Army** n/k, C garage.

TERRINGTON ST JOHN – Free Methodist 1845, U, *.

THEMELTHORPE – Primitive Methodist n/k, X.

This small Free Methodist chapel at Stoke Ferry, now converted to a garage, was built in 1860. A Wesleyan chapel also survives, converted to a house, and the 1851 Census also records Primitive Methodist and Quaker congregations in the village.

Gothic architecture, usually associated with town chapels, was also being adopted by village congregations by the end of the nineteenth century. Stokesby Primitive Methodist chapel of 1907 was designed by A.F.Scott, a well respected Norwich architect.

...tton, Primitive Methodist. Date stones and names of chapels ...pear in many styles and forms. Redundant chapels have often had ...eir names and denominations officially erased, yet the stone itself ...mains to provide confirmation of the chapel's existence.

THETFORD – Earl St Independent/ Congregational 1817, U. **King St Baptist** 1863, U. **Baptist** 1964, U. **Tanner St Wesleyan** 1830, additions 1984, U. **Magdalen St Salvation Army** 1911.

THOMPSON, POCKTHORPE – Primitive Methodist 1860, C house.

THORNAGE – n/k, **?Baptist**, C store.

THORNHAM – Wesleyan 1870, U, *.

THORPE MARKET – Methodist 1905, C store.

THORPE ST ANDREW – Undenominational C20, U. **Gospel Hall** C20, U.

THURLTON – United Methodist Free 1856, C house.

THURNE – Primitive Methodist 1971 on site of chapel built 1852, U, *.

THURSFORD – Methodist 1934, U, *.

TIBENHAM – Primitive Methodist/Wesleyan erected 1848, rebuilt 1899, architect H.Winkworth, Ipswich, U, *.

TILNEY ALL SAINTS – Wesleyan n/k, C house 1968.

TILNEY ST LAWRENCE – Primitive Methodist 1. 1897, C carpenter and undertaker, *. **2. (At Fen End)** 1870, U, *.

TITTLESHALL – Baptist (Particular) 1823, manse added, C house. **Primitive Methodist** 1865, extended 1878, U, *.

TIVETSHALL ST MARGARET – Society of Friends founded 1674, rebuilt 1811, closed 1937, C house.

TIVETSHALL ST MARY – Wesleyan 1860, C store.

TOFT MONKS, MAYPOLE GREEN – Primitive Methodist 1873 (rebuild of chapel 1848), X.

TOPCROFT – Congregational 1898, architect E.Boardman, C, *.

TOTTENHILL – Primitive Methodist 1881, X, *.

TRIMINGHAM – Primitive Methodist 1909, C house.

TRUNCH – Primitive Methodist 1852, C garage. **Methodist** 1937, U, *.

TUNSTEAD – Methodist (probably Wesleyan) n/k, C barn. **Undenominational** n/k, X.

TUTTINGTON – Wesleyan Reform 1919, C store, *.

UPTON – Primitive Methodist school 1878, chapel 1891, U, *.

UPWELL – Baptist 1844, school 1911 architect W.H.H.Davis, U.

UPWELL, LAKESEND – Primitive Methodist 1914, U.

UPWELL, THREE HOLES – Wesleyan Reform Methodist 1850 , X, *.

WACTON – Wesleyan c1895, U.

The old Baptist chapel at Tittleshall is now converted to two houses. This date stone on the end gable, hidden in a bedroom of a house built abutting on the chapel, provides proof of the original use of the building.

WALPOLE ST ANDREW, WALPOLE CROSS KEYS – Primitive Methodist 1911, architect J.Kerridge, X, *.

WALPOLE HIGHWAY – Primitive Methodist 1901, X.

WALPOLE ST PETER, WALPOLE ISLAND – Primitive Methodist n/k, C house, *.

WARHAM – Primitive Methodist 1872, X.

WATLINGTON – Wesleyan n/k, C house, *. Primitive Methodist n/k, C antique shop.

WATTON – Congregational 1856, U, *. Methodist 1926, U, *.

WEASENHAM ALL SAINTS – Primitive Methodist c1857, C house.

WELLINGHAM – United Free Methodist 1897, C house.

WELLS NEXT THE SEA – Independent 1816, enlarged 1826, school 1891, U. Society of Friends founded 1697, meeting-house 1783, extended 1913, U, *. Wesleyan 1808, C public library, *. Primitive Methodist 1891, U, *.

WELNEY – Primitive Methodist 1890, C builders' merchant, *.

WELNEY, TIPS END – Baptist 1873, architect .Kerridge, X.

WENDLING – Primitive Methodist 1. 1877, C shop, . 2. 1914, U, *.

WEREHAM – Wesleyan 1. 1844, C house. 2. new building next door, n/k, C house.

WESTFIELD – Primitive Methodist 1876, C house, *.

WEST ACRE – Primitive Methodist 1887, architect .F. Scott, C store.

WEST DEREHAM – Primitive Methodist 1903, X, *.

WEST LYNN – Wesleyan 1870, altered 1985, U, *.

WEST RAYNHAM – Wesleyan 1875, U.

WEST RUNTON – Methodist 1951, U.

WEST WALTON – Free Methodist 1849, U.

WEST WINCH – Primitive Methodist 1874, X.

WEYBOURNE – Primitive Methodist 1904, U, *.

WHINBURGH – Primitive Methodist 1861, C garage, *.

WHISSONSETT – Primitive Methodist 1903, X.

WHITWELL – Primitive Methodist 1831, C house.

WICKHAMPTON – Wesleyan 1813, X.

WICKLEWOOD – Primitive Methodist n/k, closed 1942, C house.

WICKMERE – Primitive Methodist 1897, C village hall.

WIGGENHALL ST GERMAN – Wesleyan 1860, C workshop, *. Primitive Methodist 1902, U, *.

WIGGENHALL ST MARY MAGDALENE – Baptist (General) 1840, C band hall. Primitive Methodist – 1862, altered 1985, U, *.

WIGGENHALL ST MARY THE VIRGIN, SADDLEBOW – Wesleyan 1886, X. Primitive Methodist 1910, architect J.M. Kerridge, U, *.

WIGHTON – Primitive Methodist 1874, U, *.

WILBY – Primitive Methodist 1851, C house.

WIMBOTSHAM – Primitive Methodist 1874, school 1896, closed 1934, reopened and altered 1950, 1970, U. United Methodist c1845, C house, *.

WINFARTHING – Primitive Methodist 1904, architect H. Winkworth, C house, *.

WINTERTON – Primitive Methodist 1876, U, *.

WITTON – Primitive Methodist 1865, C house 1968.

WIVETON – United Free Methodist n/k, C house.

WOOD DALLING – Independent/Wesleyan Reform 1820, C 1990 house. Primitive Methodist 1836, U. Salvation Army c1900, C house.

WOOD NORTON – Primitive Methodist c1890, C house.

WOODTON – Wesleyan c1840, C house. Primitive Methodist 1836, U.

WORMGAY – Primitive Methodist 1862, C garage, *.

WORSTEAD – Primitive Methodist 1892, C store.

WORSTEAD, MEETING HILL – Baptist (Particular) 1829 replaced earlier chapel, U, *.

WORTWELL – Independent/Congregational 1773, U, *. **Baptist** 1822, U as RC Church.

WRENINGHAM – Methodist 1906, U.

WYMONDHAM – Friars Croft Baptist meeting formed 1796, C house. **Baptist** 1909, U, *. **Independent/Congregational** 1715, altered 1815, 1876/8, new front 1910. U. **Society of Friends** 1687, altered 1800, C house 1950. **Wesleyan** 1879, C 1932 Masonic Temple, *. **Primitive Methodist 1. Norwich Rd** 1844, C house. **2. Town Green** 1870, altered 1875, U. **Salvation Army 1.** late C19, C shop and store. **2.** 1950, closed 1970, C store. **Plymouth Brethren** 1848, C house,*.

WYMONDHAM, SILFIELD – Primitive Methodist 1866, C house, *.

WYMONDHAM, SUTON STREET – Primitive Methodist 1899, U.

WYMONDHAM, SPOONER ROW – Wesleyan 1813, schoolroom 1881, refronted and altered 1949, X.

YAXHAM – Congregational 1875, U. **United Free Methodist** 1860, U.

Martham Baptist Chapel 1879.

Cromer Baptist Chapel 1901.

East Rudham Primitive Methodist 1862.